THE BOOK OF LETTERS
I didn't know where to send

STEVE PATTERSON

The Book of
LETTERS
I Didn't Know Where to Send

GOOSE LANE

Edited by Martin Townsend.
Cover and page design by Julie Scriver.
Cover image by John Hryniuk Photography.
Printed in Canada.
10 9 8 7 6 5 4 3

Library and Archives Canada Cataloguing in Publication

Patterson, Steve, 1971-, author
    The book of letters I didn't know where to send / Steve Patterson.

Issued in print and electronic formats.
ISBN 978-0-86492-883-2 (paperback).--ISBN 978-0-86492-956-3 (epub).
--ISBN 978-0-86492-957-0 (mobi)

    1. Letters--Humor. 2. Canadian wit and humor (English). I. Title.

PN6231.L44P38 2016   C818'.602   C2016-902288-9
                                       C2016-902289-7

Goose Lane Editions acknowledges the generous support of the Government of Canada, the Canada Council for the Arts, and the Government of New Brunswick.

Goose Lane Editions
500 Beaverbrook Court, Suite 330
Fredericton, New Brunswick
CANADA E3B 5X4
www.gooselane.com

To my wife Nancy and daughter Scarlett.
If enough people laugh at this book, I'll be home more often.

Contents

Dear reader,

I have always liked the concept of letters. Both the ones that combine to make words and the ones that are collections of words that make people do things (like read, for instance).

I'm not exactly sure what the first letter I wrote consisted of, but I probably wrote it around the age of 9. Something to the effect of...

> Dear Mom,
> Gone out. Back later.
> Love,
> Anonymous

I've progressed quite a bit since then. But the basic formula for me has always been the same:

1. Address your audience.

2. Convey essentially truthful but not overly specific information.

3. Leave them laughing.

It's a very similar formula in successful standup comedy. To make people in a room laugh, you need to quickly let them know who you are, let them know you know who they are and then say things that make you laugh so that they are laughing *with* you.

This is not to say mimes can't be funny. They just write awful letters.

So it is that I wrote my first comedy letter shortly after embarking on my first comedy tour across Canada. Faced with countless hours in hotel rooms, I had to "use what I had," and what I had in every room were notices, letters if you will, concerning energy conservation and towel washing. The irony of cardboard notices urging people to conserve wherever possible struck me as ridiculous and hilarious at the same time.

So I wrote my own little letter in response. The first time I read it on stage, it immediately struck a chord with every member of the audience who had stayed in a lot of hotels, and it contained enough information that those who hadn't could still be in on the joke.

Now, a scant 17 years later, I've been encouraged to assemble a collection of letters (which, remember, are in themselves collections of letters) into a book. Some of these I've shared on stage. Most I haven't. You'll enjoy some more than others. If you're a minivan driver or a Republican, you should probably just stop reading right now. I'll wait here...

OK, if you're still with me, thanks for staying. I really do hope you enjoy reading these letters as much as I have enjoyed writing them. Whether you do or not, I encourage you to write me a letter about it.

Yours truly,
Steve Patterson

PS: I take back what I said about minivan drivers earlier. For some family travel situations it really is the most logical choice. But you Republicans have no excuse.

The Book of
LETTERS
I Didn't Know Where to Send

Dear hotels,

Can you imagine how many trees are killed every day in order to make YOUR "save the towels" notices?

Why not just tell the front desk staff to tell guests what to do with the towels? Every single person who checks in MUST talk to the front desk. Surely they could remind people verbally rather than printing out MILLIONS of PAPER reminders encouraging environment-saving conservation.

You might also consider discontinuing the cardboard notices telling me the name of my housekeeper. It really isn't imperative that I know who is cleaning my room. It's not going to make me any less messy.

Quite frankly, when she knocked on my door this morning, at <u>7:00 a.m.</u>, and said "Housekeeping!" and I replied, "Come right in, Maria. I'm waiting for you"...well, I think it made us both a little uneasy.

So I'll tell you what. If you cut down on YOUR environmental waste, I promise you I won't even shower ONCE while I'm here.

Yours truly,
Steve Patterson

PS: You won't have to worry or complain ever again about washing the towels in this room...I'm taking them with me.

Dear arseholes,

As someone who hopes he is not designated as one of you, I'm writing to ask you to stop doing what you're doing.

What are you doing, you ask?

I think you know. But in case you don't, here's my definition:

> **Arsehole (n):** A person, animal or inanimate object that exhibits narcissistic, destructive, soul-sucking behaviour with little to no regard for others. *Examples:* Investment advisor who embezzles clients' funds, bird that flies over caged animals at a zoo and taunts them, hammer that strikes my thumb instead of the nail.

This type of behaviour has a simple, specific name. It is known as "Type A." (For those who have heard this term and wondered, "What does the A stand for?"...well, now you know. You're welcome.)

We all know our fair share of Type A's. In fact, we ALL exhibit this type of behaviour from time to time. For me it's usually when I am driving in traffic. But in fairness, it's only because someone else exhibited more Type A behaviour immediately before I did.

The important thing is to offset your Type A behaviour with friendly, or "Type F," behaviour.

You see, I believe we are all on something I call the "F–A Continuum," where the 2 ends represent the aforementioned types of behaviour. Our job, as civilized human beings, is to stay towards the F side of this continuum — because if too many people veer towards the A side, we're left in a spiralling vortex of negativity that could lead to the very downfall of civilization. Example: Hitler was 125% Type A. Vladimir Putin is hovering right around 100%. Donald Trump is in the high 90s. Canada's own Stephen Harper is firmly entrenched in the mid-80s.

And all Canadian senators, politicians and so-called "professionals" who knowingly deceive others are right up there as well.

But you should know that those of us who strive to stay on the F side of the continuum will overcome.

(Note to the Type F's reading this: It's important to not be 100% Type F all the time. We've all met those people who are so friendly that all we can think to ourselves is "What an arsehole!")

You Type A's believe yourselves to be invincible, and unfortunately your behaviour is often rewarded with ever-increasing designations of power, presumably by other Type A's, who are confident they will always stay firmly "above" their fellow arseholes.

But you should be warned (because I believe myself to be a Type F) that this never happens. Eventually all Type A's turn on each other. How could you not? It's in your nature. Then you're caught in a never-ending downward spiral that will lead to a lonely and worthless existence...

(I'm not going to lie to you. At this point, this letter isn't very funny.)

But fear not, arseholes, because you do have time to save yourselves.

How?

By simply exhibiting Type F behaviour whenever possible. Hold the door open for the person behind you. Wait until you're finished with the 37-second elevator ride to talk loudly on your cell phone about things no one else could possibly care about. If you're a billionaire, disperse millions of those billions to groups that truly need it because it will truly help (and not simply for the tax break).

And for those of us who veer towards the A side of the F–A Continuum whenever an arsehole veers into your lane in traffic, take a deep breath and allow that person to continue on unabated instead of laying on the horn and/or punching a hole in the windshield from the inside. (It's not important how I know this is possible.)

It won't be easy at first. There is a lot of Type A behaviour out there. But the less you put out there, the less you'll get back. And if all of us just focus on being a little more Type F and a little less Type A every day, the world will become be a more pleasant place to live in.

Unless you really, really want to be alone. In which case, enjoy being an arsehole into a mirror.

Yours truly,
Steve Patterson
Recovering Type A

Dear cyclists,

I understand that you are excited to be taking part in a sport that requires less exertion than many others. I get that you enjoy the feeling of passing those who are jogging with a little smirk on your face, as if you are more athletic than we are.

Overall, I think that cycling is really good.

But cycling OUTFITS are really not.

Just because you technically can SAUSAGE yourself into a skin-tight suit which illustrates what Catwoman would look like if she were a middle-aged man doesn't mean you SHOULD. And as for your little shoes that attach to your pedals AND make that ever-so-irritating clippity-clop noise when you get off your bike and walk around a café (like an arsehole), as far as I can tell, those just ensure that if your bike is in an accident, you are staying with your bike throughout that accident.

Meanwhile, men, I'm just going to come right out and say it... Those shorts are revolting enough from the back. But for the love of God, COVER UP THE FRONT! No one wants to see that. Particularly not little kids out for a casual bike ride, whose parents now have to explain why "the scary man is trying to suffocate the Pokémon in his pants."

And finally, easy on the sponsorship there, OK, human billboard? You're riding through a public park on a Tuesday afternoon; you are not in the Tour de France. No one wants to look at you. And trust me, none of the companies you are "advertising" want to be associated with THAT look.

So, for the sake of common sense, common eyesight and the common good, ixnay on the overpriced, gaily coloured, crotch-hugging, over-sponsored, clippity-clops. Put on a sensibly priced T-shirt, shoes that will avoid people wanting to throw hot coffee in your face at the café and some shorts which leave your religion up to interpretation.

Yours truly,
Steve Patterson
Casual cyclist in breathable clothing

October 22, 2015

Dear Prime Minister Justin Trudeau,

Wow! Does that feel as weird to read as it did to type?

Probably not, given that you proved beyond all shadow of a doubt that you are indeed ready to be the prime minister of Canada. With a majority, no less! Not even the pollsters predicted that. And they are "correct" within a "very slight" margin of error almost "all the time."

In all sincerity, heartiest congratulations to you, your entire team (except maybe that Dan Gagnier guy, whose ethics appear better suited to the Conservative Party) and your entire family. Your mom, wife and children are justifiably beaming with pride. And I'm pretty sure your dad is pirouetting in the afterlife.

Your campaign of positivity, youthful energy and, in some instances, wide-eyed naivety is clearly what this country needed. To have risen so rapidly through the political ranks and pulled off a majority borders on a miracle. What, were you born on December 25 or something?

More importantly to me, you were born the same year as I was. I didn't expect someone from my birth year to be the PM of Canada for at least a couple more elections. So on the one hand, thank you for showing us Gen X-ers that anything is possible. And on the other hand, did you have to make me look so pathetically lazy by comparison? In fairness, though, I'm sure my dad wasn't as disappointed to hear the news as Brian Mulroney, who almost certainly turned to his son and said, "Really, Ben? *Etalk*?"

Since the day of your victory, much has been said and written (by people who have never been and never will be prime minister) about what you will "have to do" in the days, months and years ahead. Most of us are filled with hope that you will follow through on all your promises and that your "modest deficits" of billions of dollars will be offset by your promise to "immediately" legalize marijuana.

I offer you no advice on what you should do as prime minister. That would be like Stephen Harper giving advice on how to competently cover a Beatles song.

I simply vow to celebrate your win as appropriately as I can given your platform — by smoking marijuana while wearing a niqab and asking for more money from wealthy Canadians.

In any case, I really do wish you the absolute best of success in your reign at 24 Sussex, or as I like to call it, Trudeau: Part Deux.

Before I leave you to your work, I will say one more thing, though. It was a brilliant move you made during the last week of the campaign to simply ASK Canadians to grant you a majority. I can't believe the others didn't think of that. If you ask a Canadian for help nicely enough, the odds are they will do it. Especially Atlantic Canadians. Which could be why you SWEPT that region. Bravo, monsieur! Of all the improbable things your campaign proved, this most basic one is my favourite: ask nicely and you shall receive.

You asked us for a majority, Prime Minister Trudeau. Now you have received it. I really can't wait to see what you give us back.

Yours truly,
Steve Patterson

PS: Let's never talk about your "nice hair" again, OK?

Dear minivan drivers,

You do realize you're driving a minivan, right?

You're driving a minivan on a Canadian highway. Not a high-perform-ance racecar on an international speedway.

You have 4 cylinders in your engine and 2 children in the back seat. That thing to your right is a cup holder with room for 2 extra-large Tim Hortons cups. It's not a stick shift with overdrive.

So when I pull out to pass you in a non-child-carrying 6-cylinder sports car, kindly refrain from SPEEDING UP to the point where your entire vehicle is shaking, your kids are spilling their drink boxes and your engine is making sounds like a baby leopard running full speed wearing corduroy pants.

It's not going to stop me from passing you. It's not going to move you up in the NASCAR standings. And it's not going to impress your kids, who are just trying to enjoy *SpongeBob* on the DVD player (an episode I've already seen, by the way, or I wouldn't be passing you).

Just accept your place in the highway of life, move over and let me pass you by — just as the competitive motor racing part of your life should have by now.

Yours truly,
Steve Patterson
The object in your rear-view mirror that is angrier than he appears

Dear Santa,

It's been a long time since I've written to you — 35 years, to be exact. Sorry about that.

It's not that I stopped "believing." It's just that I've had everything that I want for quite a while now.

My family has kept the steady flow of socks and underwear streaming in. As for other clothes, I, like most reasonable men, buy them at the exact moment I realize I need them and not a moment sooner.

Am I still mad that you didn't bring me that rocket launcher I asked for when I was 7? I'd be lying if I said I wasn't. But in retrospect, probably a good call on your part.

So why am I writing you now? Well, with the world's economy on a slippery slope and more and more arseholes stealing things like money, property and identity from the non-arseholes, I think it's time for you to take another look at your ideas of what is "naughty" and what is "nice."

How about this? For those who have been honest and friendly (Type F's), who have earned their own money, paid their fair share and never knowingly taken anything that didn't rightfully belong to them, that's nice. Same goes for every innocent child asking for a small token of a gift, or better yet, kids who ask you to help out OTHER kids. These fine humans are the new nice, Santa.

Meanwhile, those who have willfully deceived others out of their money and have failed to spread their wealth around to others in need and/or have wasted taxpayer and media time by being vacuous vermin with the IQ of a watermelon and the body-mass index of a water buffalo, that's naughty. Also, children who are in danger of following in their parents' footsteps down that path, who don't just ask but DEMAND things — they're naughties too.

Not only should the naughty people NOT get presents, but you should consider dropping a St. Nick–sized dose of reindeer dung on them from way up in the sky. Sure, some of them would try to sue you (many of them are lawyers), but I've seen enough Christmas movies to know that you'll figure out a way to avoid jail time.

Hence, what you will have left on your nice list will be every wide-eyed child and adult who needs the hope that you can bring. I know that's how it used to work. But as the distance between the "haves" and "have-nots" continues to widen, I really can't think of a better guy than you to bridge the gap and remind us what Christmas is all about. Except, I guess, maybe Jesus Christ. So I'll write Him next.

Yours truly,
Steve Patterson

Dear Jesus Christ,

I've spoken to you many times, but since I still haven't received an official reply, I thought I'd try writing.

Full disclosure: I've also written a letter to your dad. (I mean God, not Joseph. I was asking about divine intervention, not woodworking.)

In any case, my question pertains mainly to your teenage years here on Earth. As a practicing Catholic who has attended a LOT of masses (or is the plural just "mass," like "fish"?) and heard many readings from the Bible (I've read passages myself too, but isn't it always more enjoyable when someone else reads it?), I can't seem to remember hearing much, if anything, about your formative adolescent years.

I'm familiar, as most are, with the story of your birth, which seems extremely foreign to me considering the excellent state of health care where I live. (A manger? Come on! They wouldn't even let us leave the hospital until we showed them we had an up-to-code car seat.) And of course I am familiar with the tragic story of your death. That Pontius Pilate was a prick. Period. And those Roman soldiers can go to hell (and probably did).

But what about the teenage years, growing up as the Lord, Jesus Christ? The ACTUAL Lord, not a meaningless title like the British give to old guys. I can only imagine the friction between you and your folks.

Most teenagers think they're the Lord anyway. But you actually were!... Sorry. ARE!

I imagine you coming home from school and running right across the pond, just showing off for your friends, then your mom Mary yelling at you from the front door:

"JESUS CHRIST! I TOLD YOU NOT TO DO THAT!"

Then you, responding as any teenager would:

"WHAT?"

Then Mary sending you to your room, saying, "You wait until your dad gets home!"

Then you, defiantly, "He's not even my REAL dad!"

Then doors slamming everywhere — or at least curtains being aggressively drawn. (I'm not sure the traditional household door was in use back then. Particularly not in mangers.)

I know it sounds facetious, but as a teenager going to church, I always wondered, "Would teenage Jesus have to put up with what I do? Pimples? Girls' rejections? Not being a good skater?" (Sure, you could WALK on water. But how much ice was there to practice on in Bethlehem?)

All I'm saying is, teenagers can all use positive role models, Jesus. Positive TEENAGE role models. If you were the anti–Justin Bieber of your time, I'd like to hear about it so I can pass it on.

Faithfully yours,
Steve Patterson #3323

PS: That whole story about you angrily overturning tables in the temples, that was in your 20s right? Otherwise, I'm sure Mary would totally have grounded you.

Dear letter A,

I like you. I like you a lot. You start many sentences, periods and even books. When doubled, you help alcoholics. When tripled, you help stranded motorists in America. When quadrupled, you help many pizza companies become the first listing in the phone directory.

You stand alone as the logo for the Atlanta Braves. You let people know that Aquaman is near. Hell, you even let things be known as something else when you separate yourself using my nemesis, the letter K, as in "a.k.a."

I don't think there is much I could suggest to improve on you, letter A. You are first in the alphabet, first in the <u>word</u> "alphabet" and first in the choice of letters that can, in themselves, be words.

You are also the best grade that a person can get, be it student, piece of meat or student piece of meat.

I guess the one qualm I have with you is your inclusion in derogatory terms such as the word "arsehole."

They should find another letter to start that word, as well as its more crass cousin, "asshole." Why must you be the beginning of that term, my sweet letter A? Though here in Canada, we balance that out by saying what you sound like at the end of many of our sentences... eh?

CANADA has always been there for you. That's why you are in our country's name 3 times as much as any other letter. I will always consider you one of my favourite letters, if not my ABSOLUTE favourite, and argue against any of the other letters on your behalf. Or I guess, technically, on you're A-half.

Yours truly,
Steve Patterson

PS: When placed after the letters "PS," you are a public service announcement, which is also nice.

Dear opponents of same-sex marriage,

Let me just clarify something here. Same-sex marriage laws make the act of marrying the same sex <u>legal</u>. Not <u>mandatory</u>. OK?

Those of you who wish to marry the opposite sex may still do so. Those of you currently married to the opposite sex don't have to switch.

And notice the term "same-sex." It doesn't necessarily mean gay.

In fact, same-sex marriage may be the perfect solution not just for loving gay couples but also for straight men and women who haven't yet found their soulmate through "traditional relationships."

For instance, say I got married to my buddy Ted. Sure, we wouldn't be able to have kids biologically. But I would argue that many couples who do have kids biologically shouldn't. So it balances out. Plus, several children awaiting adoption are far better off with 2 loving parents in a stable home environment than zero loving parents in a non-stable environment — children, by the way, who are far more advanced in their thinking than you.

Plus, if I married Ted, I would honestly be marrying my best friend instead of just saying "I married my best friend," like other people do.

No heterosexual marriage is ever between "best friends." There are just certain things a man can say to his real <u>best friend</u> that he cannot say to his wife. Things like "Look at the rack on her," or "No, you're wrong."

Most importantly, we wouldn't have to waste valuable wedding money on useless imported items like fine china and silver. If I married Ted, we would register at the liquor store and the Ferrari dealership. Period.

Yours truly,

Steve Patterson

PS: To those that yell "It's Adam and Eve, not Adam and Steve," how would you know whom all "Steves" are attracted to?

Dear quotation marks in advertising,

I think you are just "great." I "really" do.

From saying something is the "best" to promising it is "new and improved," you guys have really found an interesting way to indicate when things are the exact opposite of what you are writing.

So who is your target market anyway? People who can read letters but can't read punctuation? Or people with a genetic disorder preventing them from seeing quotation marks?

It irks me because I used to work as an advertising copywriter, and I know a lot of the tricks that are used. Such as advertising a car with the largest engine compartment as a ratio of its total body dimension as "biggest engine in its class." Or claiming a beer is brewed with "ice cold mountain glacier water," when I know for a fact that it was brewed in London, Ontario, where there is nary a steep hill, let alone a "mountain glacier."

At what point did quotation marks become a free pass for blatantly false advertising?

You are like a lawyer in court who says something horrible and then, by adding the word "withdrawn," acts as if those words weren't even said:

> LAWYER 1: Your Honour, this man is a filthy, lying prick, and he's probably riddled with STDs!
>
> LAWYER 2: Objection!
>
> LAWYER 1: Withdrawn.

I don't get it. I don't like it. I much preferred when you guys just indicated actual quotes.

There. I said it.

Yours truly,
Steve Patterson
Big "fan" of false advertising

Dear baseball,

I like you.

I used to play you a lot as a kid growing up, and now as a grown man I appreciate watching you be played by young millionaires (when the major league playoffs are on and the Toronto Blue Jays are in them).

I understand the inner workings of baseball strategy, much as my dad does when he yells at the television, "THIS GUY DOESN'T KNOW WHAT HE'S DOING!"

What I don't understand is the concept of baseball uniforms.

From the traditional baseball cap, which flies off whenever people run — which is, granted, rare in your sport — down to the metal spiked shoes, which I could understand if your players got into a ninja fight, but that happens even more rarely than running.

Most confusing, though, has to be the fact that your coach or "manager," unlike in any other sport, ALSO wears a full team uniform. Why? Is there a chance that, should one of the players get hurt (likely from a sunflower seed going "down the wrong pipe"), you will call on a portly, elderly man to take his place?

Matter of fact, not only does your coach not need to wear a uniform, nobody does! Baseball is the easiest game in the world when it comes to identifying who is on which team. The guys standing around on the field, reminding one another how to count up to 3, that's the defensive team. The other guys, wearing helmets and waving sticks that make contact with the ball less than 30% of the time, are the other team. This is super clear to me.

It would make the game a lot more interesting to watch if you just let everyone wear whatever they wanted. The veteran designated hitter could arise from his nap every 3 innings in a pair of wrinkle-free Dockers with a cardigan draped over his Tommy Bahama shirt. The mobility-challenged first baseman could lumber onto the field in a muumuu. And the ludicrously recompensed relief pitchers could wear ludicrously tight Speedos since they spend most of the day sunning themselves in the bullpen anyway.

Everyone could still wear belts but would be encouraged to get witty novelty buckles with messages like "Baseball is for swingers," or "My other belt buckle is a pie plate."

Then, at least, there would be something to look at during the ample portions of downtime during a baseball game instead of a bunch of men in matching short-sleeved pantsuits, standing or sitting around idly chewing and spitting, like so many cows in a field.

Yours truly,
Steve Patterson
Bona fide Blue Jays fan, just wondering what's up with the wardrobe

Dear 9-year-old self,

I know life is weird right now. Your parents have just gotten divorced, your 16-year-old brother Ross is very tough (so "play fights" aren't going well), and you spend a lot of time playing baseball by yourself (which isn't easy).

I could tell you that life is "going to get better," but that wouldn't be completely true.

On the bright side, you're going to fall in love...with girls...who will love you back. Which I know doesn't seem possible right now because they laugh at you for playing baseball with yourself. Plus you don't really "like" girls yet. (Trust me, that WILL change.)

You will get your driver's licence one day, so you won't have to ride your bike everywhere, which will be great. But you'll spend a good deal of that "driving time" stuck in traffic, wishing you were riding your bike.

Are your parents going to get back together? Unfortunately not. Yes, you were technically the "save the marriage" baby, and the marriage wasn't saved. But trust me, it's not your fault. If you have any friends who tell you their parents are "staying together for the kids," tell them to advise their parents, "Thanks, but no thanks."

Will you become a professional baseball player? I hate to tell you this, but no. Still, this doesn't mean you should spend any less time playing baseball right now. You love it. Keep doing it. Plus, "thinking about baseball" is going to come in handy during another activity that you'll be engaging in starting about 9 years from now, which you're going to learn to love a lot more than baseball.

Are you ever going to win a fight against your brother? Nope. He will always be bigger and stronger than you — though at some point you might be able to take down your 2 oldest brothers (but as of the writing of this letter, that moment hasn't arrived).

You're going to lose people in your life you thought would be there forever. You're going to fall out of love almost as many times as you fall into it. Some of your dreams that you work very hard towards are not going to come true.

But then, some things you never expected to happen are going to amaze you.

For instance, that kid you just met across the street, Ted? He's going to be your best friend for the rest of your life. Something that people will eventually call "BFF." (It sounds dumb, I know. The world actually gets dumber in the future.)

Your buddy Jeff that you just started playing baseball with (which is much easier than by yourself, by the way), he's also going to be in your life for years and years to come. Matter of fact, both of these pals will stand beside you at your wedding.

That's right, little self, you're going to get married. To a girl who is only one year old right now, which, when I put it that way, seems gross. But it makes sense many years from now.

And you're going to be a dad. True story! To a beautiful little girl that you and your wife, Nancy (there's a hint), will name Scarlett.

Those 2 girls are going to become the most important people in your life. Because family is more important than anything, self. It might not seem that way now, but believe me, never pass up a chance for family time. You'll regret it later. A lot.

So what are you going to become? A doctor? A lawyer? A politician, maybe? No, no and no (though you will get to be student council president at your high school — which I probably shouldn't have told you).

I'm not going to tell you what you're going to become because that would ruin the journey of trying as many things as you can until you find the one thing that you love to do. That's the best part, self: you get to do what you love for a job.

All in all, you really are a lucky young man, Stephen. (Sorry. I know you hate being called Stephen.) So enjoy life! Stay on the right side of the law, but don't forget to live a little or you will bore yourself to death. Yes, that CAN happen.

Oh, and if you get a chance to make somebody laugh, give it a shot. You never know where that might lead.

Yours truly,
Future you

Dear missing socks,

I'm not sure this letter will ever reach you, but if it does…WHAT THE HELL HAPPENED?

Each of you went into the washing machine with your identical twin. There is no way to escape from that machine. Then you were transferred to the dryer, which is also airtight.

Were you dropped on the floor during the transfer?

I don't think so, or I would have…*wait for it*…picked you up and thrown you in the next dryer load.

Once dried and fabric-softened, your identical twin emerged, smelling far better than when he went in. (I'm not trying to be sexist here. I am a male and I assume my socks are male socks. No female sock would put up with my feet.)

But you were nowhere to be found!

When this happened at public laundromats in my younger days, I just assumed some freak with a sock fetish was going into the dryer when I would leave and taking odd numbers of socks. Why he didn't take BOTH, I always wondered. But hey, if you're weird enough to take socks from laundromats, you're weird enough to not take matching pairs.

Now, however, I do my laundry at <u>home</u>. The entire house is locked as tight as the washing machine. No one is breaking into my home, stealing socks and then leaving. How do I know for sure? I've sat by the front door and watched, that's why. I'm not an idiot.

So, I'm asking you directly, what the hell happened? Was there a fight between you and your twin, like Cain and Abel, and you came out on the Abel end of things (which is to say, you didn't come out)? Because if so, I've been harbouring a murderer for a while now and could be considered an accessory. (Though technically, I guess, the sock is the accessory.)

I don't expect an answer. I hope that somehow you "escaped" or simply left to live out the rest of your days on someone else's foot, perhaps even a one-footed person's foot, in which case, you have indeed "gone to a better place."

I suppose there's no point in all those missing sock posters I've put up around my neighbourhood.

But on the off-chance that you do read this (and can even READ, considering that you're a sock), please know that you are missed. I appreciate all the time you spent keeping my foot warm. And I've learned my lesson. Any socks I don't want to LOSE from now on, I simply will not WASH.

    Yours truly,
    Steve Patterson
    Man who often wears un-matching socks

Dear news panel "experts,"

Forgive me, but I don't have much faith in your expertise.

Because if you were actually "experts," I would think you would be in such high demand in your field of expertise that you wouldn't be available to comment on the news nightly.

You are most often called upon to form an "expert political panel." However, people who are not and have never been employed in politics and appear as "experts" on news panels might as well just be senior citizens at the local coffee shop who believe that their way is right and any other way is wrong, and who also don't have anyone actually in politics offering them a job.

The most perplexing type of news experts to me, though, are the "terrorist experts." I don't mean the military personnel who have actually been to war or who are still fighting terrorism on a daily basis. No, I mean someone who has read a lot about terrorism, then written a book about terrorism based on what they have *read* and then decided to appear on the news as a terrorism expert.

Actual terrorism experts are terrorists. Period.

I'm certainly not saying they are correct or wise. I'm simply saying they are actively invested and they generally don't share the knowledge they have amassed with news panels.

Of course there are also "counter-terrorists," who need to know enough about terrorism to effectively battle the terrorists and keep the rest of us safe. Bless these people, but I would prefer they spend all their time monitoring terrorists and not identifying themselves.

In any case, I don't hold this against newscasts. It gets pretty boring just seeing and hearing that one anchorperson, even when he or she cuts to the often incorrect "meteorologist" or the wacky sportscaster. Additional faces and voices are needed and you, at least here in Canada,

have long since abandoned the idea of bringing on well-spoken entertainers who might, God forbid, *entertain* viewers while simultaneously
informing them.

But I think that calling people who are not quite good enough to actually be employed in an industry "experts" is akin to calling the retail clerks
who work in an Apple computer store and have a working knowledge
of computers "geniuses."

Good talk.

Yours truly,
Steve Patterson
"Comedy Expert"

Dear St. Patrick,

You are my favourite St.

Not just because mention of your name usually conjures up images of a fun-filled day and night and next morning of people drinking beer, singing (badly) and pretending to be Irish, but also because of the complexity of your character.

For instance, I have always associated you with ridding Ireland of snakes. This fascinates me because I didn't know the climate of Ireland was suitable for even a single snake to survive in, let alone enough of them to be considered an infestation. It must be true, though, because this is how I and many others know you, and it wouldn't have been like my Irish ancestors to just "make something up."

But upon further research (I Googled your name and was sent to "catholic.org"), I learned that you were born in Scotland to Roman parents around the year 385. So the person the entire world equates with drinking in Irish pubs is...a Scottish-Italian hybrid? Weird.

Furthermore, you were taken to Ireland as a slave at the age of 14 and kept in captivity until the age of 20, when a dream from God told you to leave Ireland by going to the coast. Really? It took you 6 years to realize that, when being held captive on an island, it might be a good idea to head to the coast for your best chance at escape?

Then in another dream the people of Ireland called out to you to come back...so you did? What was it about being a slave for 6 years that brought you back? The lack of freedom or the discipline of a steady routine?

Somehow in all of this you became a priest, then a bishop, and converted Ireland to Christianity, preaching the Gospel for over 40 years and living in poverty and much suffering until you died on March 17 in the year 461. Well, I'm not going to lie to you, St. Patrick. That story SUCKS. You died penniless and suffering after spreading the word of the Gospel for 40 years in a place where you had previously been held captive and that you had successfully escaped?

Your behaviour is no doubt saintly. But you'd be forgiven for not looking back kindly on your Irish experience, given that you weren't even FROM there in the first place.

And as for the snakes, WTH, St. P.? Turns out the "snakes" were just symbols of paganism. They can't migrate across water. That's science.

So all of this talk about "snakes" and "charming snakes" and "look how great a job St. Patrick did because we've been snake-free for as long as anyone can remember" is a bunch of bollocks. There are no snakes, never were. But there are still a few pagans, mostly from England, who go to Dublin for their bachelorette parties to this very day.

It seems dishonest. It seems an affront to the commandment "Thou shalt not lie." But do I disagree enough to stop drinking on St. Patrick's Day? Hell no!

This is just so you know, St. Patrick — IF that's your real name, which I know it wasn't (depending on where you look, it was either "Maewyn" or "Kevin"; I'm pulling for Maewyn) — WHATEVER YOUR NAME IS, I'm on to you. So I drink on St. Patrick's not to "honour" you but strictly to DIS-honour myself.

Yours truly,
Steve Patterson
Drinker of Guinness, seeker of truth

Dear The Bay,

Your stores have been around a long time, eh?

The Hudson's Bay Company, founded as a fur-trading corporation in 1670, long before Canada was even a country, is now officially <u>North America's oldest company</u>.

So congratulations on being in business this long! That's well over 300 years of transactions (while Target Canada couldn't even make it to year 2). You guys must be doing something right.

The problem is, whenever I go into one of your stores, you do everything wrong.

From the placement of ludicrously lit cosmetic counters at every conceivable entrance, to the world-class hiding ability of your employees, no trip to The Bay for me has ever been routine or enjoyable.

The last time I went in, I was shopping for underwear. Translation: I am a man, who had forgotten to pack underwear on a trip and had already worn the pair I brought inside out and then outside in (again) and then spent one day going commando. So I had to either wash my underwear or buy new ones.

To be completely honest, I wouldn't even have gone into your store for this if there had been any other viable alternative. But I was in a small city, and small cities typically don't feature men's underwear stores because small-city men buy underwear even less frequently than big-city men do (Google it).

So there I was, in the ladies' cosmetic section I had inadvertently walked into, politely refusing the kind counter lady's offer to give me a "man makeover" since she had so much makeup on herself she looked like a Kardashian had a baby with a clown. When I asked her where the men's underwear section was, she replied, and I quote, "Why would I know that?" My easy answer to that would have been to say "Because you WORK here." But clearly this woman had enough to deal with, applying that much makeup every day, so I said, "Thanks, I'll find it myself," and left that section in search of another with dimmer lighting and a brighter employee.

Eventually I found the men's underwear section. It was on the third floor, in the back corner, as far away from any entrance as possible.

I had a choice between one completely unwrapped pair of boxer shorts, which had probably already been handled more than any other pair of underwear in that town, or a pack of "tighty-whities" that came in either small or extra large. Perfect. So I had 3 options. Either my underwear was going to be "previously enjoyed" or I would be continuously pulling my underwear up from around my ankles or it was going to cut off circulation to my most valued body part.

I made a game-time decision to buy the extra-large pack. After all, I could just staple them on. Plus, there was a good chance I would eventually grow into them.

Tighty-whities in hand, I began my search for an employee to complete the purchase. It was, as it always is at your stores, like trying to play hide and seek in a house with a kid who jumped in a taxi when you started counting. After what seemed like an hour of not being able to find a single soul on the third floor (let alone a store employee), I had the idea to go back to the cosmetics counter lady from earlier. If nothing else, I could tell her where the men's underwear section was so she could pass that info on to the next man who unwittingly wandered into her section seeking rollicking repartee.

Then, a man approached. A man wearing a tie. So he either worked here or he was trying to steal a tie. I asked him if he worked there and he said, "Yeah, of course." Then I asked him, "Have you ever thought of hanging out a little closer to the cash register on the off-chance a person might come in to make a purchase?" And he said, "Sir, there's no need for that tone."

That's when I threw the package of tighty-whities at the tie-wearing idiot's head and stormed out of the store. (Once you've gone commando once, an extra day doesn't really hurt you.)

All of this to say, I probably won't be back to any of your stores any time soon.

In fact, based on this last experience, I am utterly amazed that you are still in business. I imagine it's only because you're not allowed to close because there are still men missing in your stores from over 300 years ago, desperately trying to find someone, anyone, that they can pay with their fur pelts.

Yours truly,
Steve Patterson

PS: If it makes you feel any better, I have a similar story about shopping at Sears.

Dear yoga,

On behalf of the Western world, I just want to say, "Well done!"

You apparently existed over in the old "Eastern world" (India) for a long, long time (like, 10,000 years?), but only within the last couple of decades have you really caught on over here.

Sure, there were the "early adopters" here, who would preach your merits and then <u>practice</u> what they preached. And that's what it's called, right? You "practice" yoga. You don't "play it" or simply "do" it. You practice it. Like piano. Or law. Or pretending to be sober when you're drunk.

Anyway, there are so many yoga studios in my West End Toronto neighbourhood now, with so many people "practicing," that I'd have to say you have pretty much perfected your business plan at this point. From yoga-specific clothing lines like Lululemon and...whoever else makes yoga clothing, to studios that aren't afraid to charge an arm and a leg to make you wrap your arms and legs in uncomfortable, unnatural and for many of us "unpossible" positions. All of this in pursuit of strengthening your mind AND body, finding inner peace and maybe, once you have practiced enough, being able to lick yourself clean like a cat.

I've only practiced yoga a few times myself. Once, like every young, hot-blooded university man, I tried it just to have a perfect vantage point to watch the young hot-blooded university ladies doing yoga. Once it was with a comedy club owner in Ottawa, who tried to kill me with something called "Bikram's Hot" yoga (it was like exercising inside a volcano). And most recently it was at one of the yoga studios near my house called Breathe (always a good tip) in a class called Yoga for Stiff Men (grow up!).

I actually liked the play on words (I hoped it was a play on words), so I attended 6 classes, which were full of other middle-aged men like me doing poses nowhere near how the young male instructor was instructing them. At least, I don't think they were. Unlike during my first yoga experience, I had zero incentive to look at the others in the class, and I'm sure they felt the same about me.

But I have to say that, after practicing you, I felt energized and relaxed at the same time. This is probably because each class ended with a 15-minute position called Shavasana, which is the ancient yoga word for nap. Or in the case of a Yoga for Stiff Men class, nap and fart.

I can't begin to explain how good it felt to get out of that room.

In any case, good on you, yoga, for stretching your way across the world and transforming yourself. You've gone from an ancient spiritual ritual that everyone did by themselves for free to a new-ancient spiritual ritual that people could still do by themselves for free but now pay thousands of dollars for so they can be in a room with others they never look at.

If you're at peace with yourselves for that, then so am I.

Namaste, yoga.
Nama-Steve Patterson

Dear luxury sports car drivers,

First of all, let me just say congratulations on your expensive purchase. Obviously things are going very well in your life financially and you are either a professional executive, a doctor, a professional athlete or a drug dealer, or else were simply born into a wealthy family.

In any case, nice wheels you've got there! Well done!

Having said that, could you maybe not drive like a complete and total arsehole?

Between Corvettes zipping in and out of highway traffic at high speeds and Ferraris revving louder than a hungry lion trying out his new Harley, the purchase of a luxury sports car seems to come with a lobotomy thrown in.

I don't know if you know this, but there is a feature your car has called turn signals or "indicators." They indicate to other drivers that you are going to change lanes and/or turn in front of oncoming traffic. They're extremely handy for those of us in other cars who, sadly, aren't equipped with extra-sensory perception and therefore have no way of inherently knowing when you are going to manoeuvre your car. I learned this the hard way when a man driving a Mercedes Benz turned left directly in front of me, with nary an indication whatsoever, thus totaling my car and doing a great deal of expensive damage to his. I've seen this same moronic move performed by so many luxury car drivers that it makes me wonder if maybe turn signals are a car dealership "option" that you can opt not to get, instead selecting seats made from the hides of endangered species.

Also, if you are considering buying a car that can comfortably travel at speeds in excess of 240 km/h, ask yourself a few basic questions:

1. Why? Why would I buy this car and not just buy an airplane that can go even faster and will face fewer traffic obstacles?

2. Where? Where could I conceivably drive this car to its full potential?

3. DO I LIVE NEAR ENOUGH TO THAT AREA TO DRIVE THIS CAR THERE?

These are all important questions that are apparently not asked by the many drivers I see idling in downtown traffic as I WALK past them, pointing and laughing at the person inside.

I could go on about the ludicrous maintenance charges (I think an oil change on a Jaguar costs more than it would to house and feed an actual jaguar) and the fact that luxury cars seem to be broken down on the side of the road as often or more so than non-luxury cars (this is assuming BMWs are still considered "luxury cars"), but I think I've made my point.

Then again, what do you care what I or anyone else (except women who choose to date men based on the car they drive) thinks?

Well, just in case you're wondering, it's this: "That man driving that car must have a very small penis."

Yours truly,
Steve Patterson
Man with average-size car and average-size penis

Dear Garys of the world,

I just heard that you may soon become extinct as a name since very few parents are naming their little boys Gary anymore (and for the record, even fewer parents are naming their little girls Gary).

How can this be? Gary seems like a name that should live on. Like Adam. Or Michael. Or dare I say Steve?

Gary seems like as good a name as any.

Just think of all the famous Garys there have been. Back in the late '70s and early '80s, there was the lovable Gary Coleman from *Diff'rent Strokes*, who gave us that immortal catchphrase: "What'chu talkin' 'bout, Willis?" I can't tell you how many times I've used that myself, and I've never even met anyone named Willis (so maybe THAT name is in trouble too).

The 1980s Montreal Expos had Gary "the Kid" Carter, who seemed to have as much fun playing baseball as any man has ever had doing anything. Then there are other famous actors like Gary Oldman and my personal favourite, Gary Busey, who also tried to create memorable catchphrases, but unfortunately they only made any sense to him.

Apparently, though, studies show that fewer than 500 boys born in the United States were given the name Gary in the year 2013. That's down from 38,000 in the early 1950s. In the UK only 28 boys were given the name Gary in the year 2013, down from 235 in 1996. In Canada, well, I have no idea since there are no specific statistics on this, and the question "Do you have a son named Gary?" seems like a silly, random sentence to work into a conversation at a party.

So, what can be done about this?

Well, obviously, those who are expecting baby boys and want their child to be named something that hardly any other boys will also be named in the near future can now choose Gary. Or, those of us who aren't named Gary can just freely admit that we don't care if that name becomes extinct and let it just go away as (God willing) Kanye's self-imposed "Yeezus" soon will.

Sorry, Garys. You had a good run.

Yours truly,
Steve Patterson

PS: I should point out that I also wouldn't fight for the name Steve if it were becoming extinct. I've always wanted to be known as Enrique.

Dear Pablo Picasso,

I know you probably won't read this since you died a long time ago, but I wasn't around when you were alive. Plus you'd be surprised how many people I write letters to who ARE alive and still never read them, so this is not that different.

Anyway, I just wanted to say congratulations on your illustrious career of illustrations that seems to get stronger and stronger (read: more and more profitable) as the years go by (despite the fact that you are exactly the same amount of dead).

Many people consider your works masterpieces, as evidenced by the fact that your original paintings still fetch millions of dollars at auctions. But I see you for the real genius you were: a master SALESMAN.

How else can one explain paintings that seem to have been done by a 5-year-old on a sugar high becoming world-famous? With noses sticking out of foreheads and phalluses where faces should be, you somehow made "surrealism" sexy in a way that high-school-aged boys doodling genitalia in the margins of textbooks never could.

Now there are museums devoted to you around the world and aspiring artists who want to be "the next you," studying not only your paintings but infamous quotes you left behind such as "Art is a lie that makes us realize the truth." That's some deep shit there, Pablo. Or just some shit. I like art. I work in comedy, which, like your paintings, some don't believe should be defined as art.

However, you managed to make the stuffy art world take notice by creating works that, to the naked eye, might look like just naked boobs. But these boobs were different. Because they were coming out of the woman's BACK. Brilliant! When people asked who your influences were, you replied with quotes like "Bad artists copy. Good artists STEAL." The word we have for that now is "plagiarism," and it's seen as a bad thing. But good for you for finding a more artistic way to spin it.

I could go on and on about other reasons your reputation as a master artist mystifies me, but you probably have to get back to your portrait of angels with wings coming out of their arses, so I'll close with more words attributed to you. When someone asked you, "What do you seek?" you answered, "I do not seek. I FIND."

Very confident, Pablo. Cocky even. So let me respond with words I am stealing from Yoda: "There is no try. Only DO."

I am finished trying to <u>find</u> the genius in your works. I simply <u>DO</u> not see it.

Yours truly,
Steve Patterson
More of a Group of 7 guy

Dear Prince William and Princess Kate,

You don't know me, and this letter will likely never get through to you. But on the off-chance that you have a slow day with nothing to do... Actually, come to think of it, there's a good chance you MIGHT read this.

OK, then, here I go.

William, you've put a lot of pressure on me. First of all, <u>after</u> I had set my wedding date with my then fiancée of April 29, 2011, you announced you were marrying Kate on the <u>exact same day</u>.

Thanks for that.

It's tough enough trying to fulfill your bride's dream of a perfect wedding day, one that you are paying for yourself, with no external pressure. I thought I had done a pretty good job finding an English-speaking church in the Caribbean in Saint Lucia and offering to pay for the wedding meal and drinks of anyone who could make it down. (All-inclusive resorts no longer include the wedding night dinner, by the way — in case you decide to have your next Royal wedding at a Sandals Resort.) Then, since everyone was down there for the week anyway, we decided to get married on a Friday. Because NO ONE GETS MARRIED ON A FRIDAY NORMALLY, WILLIAM!

Then you decided to get married on the same Friday.

So my wedding was compared, at every turn, with your ROYAL WEDDING. Do you have any idea how difficult that is to compete with? You guys had celebrities attending from all over the world. Elton John performed. You had "commemorative plates." Don't get me wrong... We had 34 high-quality friends and family at our wedding, and I wrote my wife her own song for our first dance (which I personally think ranks somewhere between "Candle in the Wind" and "Sad Songs Say So Much"). But you really screwed me over there! The only advantage I had at my wedding was that, if they wanted to, guests were allowed to touch my grandmother without fear of imprisonment. (In fairness, I suppose, that would depend on HOW they touched my grandmother.)

As for you, Princess Kate, since we both set off simultaneously on our marital voyages, you had to go and have baby George before we had a baby. Thanks again! Now all the pressure of the Royal wedding was back, but this time with the Royal baby.

Don't get me wrong. George is a lovely boy, and it's great that he will be the King one day (which is more than I can say for your dad, William, let's be honest). Plus he does take a lot of pressure off Harry to act responsibly, which is great for Harry.

But when the people who got married the same day as you have a baby, that puts the pressure squarely on you, specifically on your sperm, to produce a baby as well. Not that I didn't love going through the motions. But it's different when it's for the express purpose of trying to make a baby. You drink less. You "do it" more. It loses a lot of spontaneity when your wife calls dibs on every erection you get.

Still, I'm happy to report that not quite a year after the birth of your baby George, my wife gave birth to our own baby girl, Scarlett. Sure, she might never technically become a princess, but she's the princess of my heart and immediately helped me forget how much pressure you guys put on me with the aforementioned things...

Then, 7 months after our Scarlett was born, you gave birth to your second child and named the baby girl Charlotte!

I've got to be honest. You guys are really pissing me off.

Yours truly,
Steve Patterson
Technically I'm one of your subjects. Which is weird since you're my arch-nemeses.

Dear "social networking,"

Congratulations on being the most ironically termed phenomenon of the 21st century.

Sure, you can help people communicate instantly from continents away and bring light to important, historic moments. The ability to instantly share video footage has shed light on examples of appalling brutality and has also helped find missing children before it's too late.

But those things aren't just "social." That's VITAL networking.

What you are to most of the world (myself included, I'm afraid) is an excuse to not be social with fellow human beings.

In every public environment now, strangers in close proximity who might have met before you existed are now buried face-first in their phones, tablets (they're not just for Moses anymore) or other devices, "socializing" with whoever is on the other end. Or even worse, they are "trolling" for interaction. So essentially they are eavesdropping on other people who are also eavesdropping on other people, all in an effort to ignore the people who are actually in the same physical space as they are.

Of course it's not just strangers who ignore each other through you. Entire families now spend entire evenings in the same home avoiding each other. Sure, kids have done this to their parents all through the ages. But at least they used to TALK when they did it. Maybe even go outside and interact. Now, they "interact" through video games like Minecraft, "developing their hand-eye coordination skills" while their "person-person coordination skills" atrophy to such an extent they may actually forget how to interact live with other human beings.

I read a report recently (yes, it was online) that said the average human attention span is now down to about 8 seconds. By comparison the average goldfish has an attention span of about 9 seconds. So, if you want to make a strong impression on a live human now, you have

7 seconds to do it, at least 3 of which must be spent somehow prying their eyes away from their screen. This leaves you with 4 seconds to make an impression worthy of the person you are talking to so that they don't abandon you for the sanctity of their social-networking screen. That's either enough time to say "Hi, how are you?" or to simply scream at the top of your lungs, either of which will likely illicit the same indifferent response.

So what can we do about this?

I don't know. And somehow, looking for the answer online seems too ironic. I guess we could all just try saying hi to the next person we meet and see what happens from there.

But if that doesn't work, I guess it's time those of us who do wish to have a chance at being social with another living thing all sharpen up our goldfish impressions.

Yours truly,
Steve Patterson
Taking a break from writing now to go socialize

Dear mountains,

There's no questioning the majesty you hold over anyone who has ever seen you. From a great distance on the ground, you are other-worldly beacons of beauty. When driving through you (on roads), one gets a greater feeling of the sheer magnitude of your magnitudi-ness (a real word when in reference to you). When flying overhead, it's like hovering over the world's best dessert, with your snow-covered tips serving as the irresistible icing on top.

You are Mother Nature's bosom (all the better because you are 100% real).

I guess it is for this reason that I don't understand people who climb you. It just wouldn't occur to me to do so.

When asked why they do it, most mountain climbers say, "Because it is there." That's the dumbest reason I've ever heard.

Lots of things are "there" that we don't climb. Buildings, for instance. Tall flights of stairs. Really tall people. By the logic of the mountain climber, I should scale all of these things whenever they present themselves to me. Which I do not. Because they are dangerous (particularly the really tall people, who tend to get angry if you even jump on them and try to keep hold, let alone actually *climb* them).

People don't climb mountains "because they are there." They climb them to "conquer" them. To show other people that nothing can get in their way. Which is weird because, for the most part, those people have gone way out of their way to get you "in their way."

Well, I'm here to tell you, mountains, that you are safe from being "conquered" by me. I will not climb up you or ski down you. I even avoid driving through you now that I have done so already a few times, because I find the view from overhead is better and there is less chance of the airplane I am in being knocked off the road by colossal logging trucks careening down towards my rental Toyota Tercel.

I'm on your side, mountains, by staying well OFF of your sides. I will never climb you "because you are there"... because I am "here."

Yours truly,
Steve Patterson
Your friend at sea level

Dear letter B,

"To you, or not to you…" Doesn't have the same ring, does it?

Shakespeare knew what the best letter was, and that's why he chose you. And by you, I mean B.

Of all the letters that aren't the letter A, you may BE my favourite. Not just Because you Begin so many of the B-est words, but you are also an insect. Almost no other letter can say that.

You make honey. Which is delicious. You pollinate flowers, which is lovely for us to witness the by-product of (and titillating, I'm sure, for the flowers). You also get together with birds and get B-usy… which I've never truly understood, but good for you, mating with someone several times your size.

Of course, there are some negatives. B movies, for instance, aren't considered very good. B-list actors who star in those movies are considered even not gooder. And Bea Arthur is now dead.

However, I think the B positives far outweigh the B negatives. For instance, that is my blood type: B+. You are coursing through me right now as I write this, so I literally couldn't live without you. Meanwhile, let's not forget Be-yoncé because she is still alive and many would argue is a more electrifying all-around entertainer than the previously mentioned, now deceased, Bea Arthur.

"But wait, there's more!" You are also the Beginning of that phrase, which always promises something truly great. Something un-Believable, even. Like a product that would cost over $6,000 in stores but now is available for just 3 easy payments of $19.99! Son of a B, that's a great deal!

And how about cute Valentine's cards that say "BE mine"? Whimsical sayings like "BE there or BE square." Bach. Beethoven. Bon Jovi. And yes, the BEA-tles. Could music even exist without you? You're the only note brave enough to not have a black key to the right of you on the piano. Which means there's no such thing as a B-sharp. You're sharp enough already.

In summary, B, you Beautiful Bastard, you just keep doing what you're doing, my friend. Standing alone as a letter, a word or an insect, there will never BE another like you.

B-est regards,
Steve

PS: I forgot to mention the song "Let It Be," which I always sing "letter B" to. No other letter has that either!

Dear car companies,

I've noticed that every year around the end of August you release your models for the next calendar year, even though that year hasn't happened yet. I have a number of questions.

First of all, how come you get to ignore the calendar the rest of us have to live by? Apparently, to you, the months of September to December just don't exist. Do you have any idea what you're missing? (Obviously not, so I'll fill you in.)

In September there's Labour Day weekend, when everyone celebrates the end of summer with one more giant piss-up in the woods without having to go back to work on Monday. It's the most ironically named of the long weekends since no one actually does anything <u>laborious</u> during this time. However, if there were a "going-into-Labour-Day" weekend 9 months later as a <u>direct</u> by-product of this drunken debacle, well, THAT would make sense.

October brings Halloween, when you see the sheer joy in children's eyes of dressing up like a cowboy or princess and, more importantly, where normally shy women dress up as "sexy cowgirls" and "sexy princesses." I can't believe you guys don't want to see that.

Then there's Canadian Thanksgiving, when people gorge themselves on turkey, potatoes and gravy and in November, American thanksgiving, when even more people eat even more food. Why is one later than the other? Partly because Canadians are more polite and so want to give thanks <u>first</u>. And partly because Americans want to keep eating straight through to the end of the year, so those who aren't obese yet have a chance to catch up.

December? Well, that's Christmas, for God's sake! (Though some would argue that because of commercialization it's not really for God's sake anymore but more of a manufactured holiday for the retail sector to ensure that the haves keep distancing themselves from the have-nots with opulent over-consumption.) Still, again, think about the magic for the children...and the women dressed sexy again, this time as "Santa's helpers."

Finally, there's New Year's Eve! How can you not love New Year's Eve? Everyone in the world who drinks alcohol is drunk. It's the one chance the average guy gets to kiss more than one woman in public and the only chance below-average guys get to kiss a woman, period. This is your night, car guys.

But you guys don't care about all that because you've got cars to sell. Cars "from the future." Which raises one more question: if you're going to just make up that a car from a future date is ready NOW, why stop at the next calendar year? Show me what a car will look like a hundred years from now. I assume it will be a rocket, suitable for space travel, that runs only on environmentalists' tears.

Yours truly,
Steve Patterson

Dear curling,

As a proud Canadian whose athletic abilities are diminishing with age (and they weren't too hot to begin with), I am intrigued by you. How is it that you have captured the imagination of countries such as Canada, Scotland, Norway and wherever else entertainment options are limited with your game of "housework on ice"?

I would say that the pace of your game is best described as "glacial," but given the current effects of climate change, it is now actually much slower than that.

As one synopsis of your history (at royalcaledoniancurlingclub.org) notes, "It is fruitless to speculate about whether the game is Scottish in origin." Fair enough.

So I will continue with the theory that I have always held: some guy, drunk and alone in the Canadian North, realized that it was easier to skip stones on the water when it's frozen. So he invited 3 friends out onto the frozen lake, who immediately accepted the offer simply because they had never before been invited to anything. Together they realized that the rocks go farther when the ice is swept (shortly after their wives realized the brooms were missing). Then they realized that they could do all this WHILE drinking beer and that it somehow, technically, counted as "exercise." Whether or not these men were Scottish-Canadian in origin is "fruitless to speculate."

History dispensed with, we skip back to the present, where you are practiced widely across Canada, with "The Brier" being the men's championship and "The Tournament of Hearts" being the women's championship. (Turns out women enjoy time away from their husbands just as much as vice versa. Who knew?) You are also included in the Winter Olympic Games, which many may argue is a farce since you aren't a sport. But I disagree with those many. Because the Olympics also includes luging, which is, literally, lying down while gravity takes hold of your body. Compared with that, you are a veritable decathlon of physical activity.

I say all this, and yet I have found myself watching late stages of your games and yelling at my screen much as I do when I watch other sports. "Come on, CURL!" I yell, inexplicably, at a rock, while, even more inexplicably, the man or woman who threw that rock also yells at it. The "sweepers" who watch the rock closely (I know they're not really called that, but I don't know what they ARE called because royalcaledon-iancurlingclub.org told me it was fruitless to ask that question) seem torn between whether they have to sweep or not. Much as I am when my wife asks me to tidy up the kitchen. But lo and behold, sometimes that rock DOES curl. And knocks out other rocks. Points are scored! Brooms are raised! And the fans in the stands go wild! (Sometimes there are only 2 of them, but that still counts as plural.)

All in all, now that I think about it, the latter stages of one of your matches in the latter stages of a tournament are actually quite exciting. Seriously.

Now if they could just give us the "highlights" of the earlier games, instead of several full days of rocks sliding up and down ice in slow motion, I think you may be able to get and keep more people interested in your sport.

Also, would it kill you to fire T-shirts into the crowd through a cannon? Because crowds love fighting over flying T-shirts. Even if there are only 2 people in that crowd.

Yours truly,
Steve Patterson

PS: I tried curling once and cracked the ice. True story. Sorry about that.

Written one month before I married Nancy

Dear ladies of Earth,

I will soon be entering into marriage with one of you, so obviously I am fond of your kind and would like to understand you better.

I do understand the basic physiological differences. You have many parts that men don't, and the ones you have that we also have look much better on you.

I know that women can sometimes be more emotional than men, so frequent re-assurances such as "You look beautiful today" are wise to make. (Note to women reading this who are angry that I just said women are "emotional": that anger is an emotion.) Though I recently learned you should only make those comments to the specific lady you are betrothed to. All other women must now be referred to as somewhere between "butt ugly" and, in the case of extremely attractive celebrities or models, "She's all right, I guess. But that's because she's airbrushed."

What I DON'T quite understand yet are your amazing recall abilities. How IS it that you can keep track of conversations that started months or sometimes YEARS before, which you then continue without warning, such as just saying "Green," while we are watching TV, and when I say, "What are you talking about?" explaining, "I said on our first date that if we were ever to get married, I would like the bridesmaid dresses to be green. Why don't you ever listen to me?" Making me reply... "You look beautiful today."

I also don't understand the laundry directions of your clothing. Which is the main reason I don't do it. (Actually it's tied for "main reason" with the fact that I hate doing laundry.) But honestly, the one among you for whom I've attempted to do laundry a few times has managed to accumulate several hundred articles of clothing, every one of which requires its own specific washing technique. Some colours must be washed "cold." Others, "warm." Others still, at precisely the temperature of the streams in the French Alps, after having been filtered through a unicorn's uterus. Lululemon things must only be washed with each other and never too hot, despite the fact that they are always full of sweat, which I have now learned women are in fact capable of doing as well as belching and cursing, and when it comes to farting, some of you are of international rank (pun intended).

I could go into more broad categories (no pun intended there), but I fear that even by joking "no pun intended" I have now offended you collectively and you will form one giant empowered woman in the shape of Oprah Winfrey and strike me down.

So I'll just conclude with this: Ladies of Earth...you are...perfect just the way you are. Or at least the one of you that I'm about to marry is.

Yours truly,
Steve Patterson
Respecter of all women, lover of one above all others

Dear Apple computers,

Well, congratulations! You've done it. You have officially brainwashed me.

As I write this on my Mac laptop listening to iTunes music on my iPad through my Apple headphones and occasionally checking messages on my iPhone, I have just written a letter to your former arch-rival, Microsoft, asking them how they are still in business.

You, on the other hand, are the most profitable company in the world. You have more money in cash reserves than many countries do. Your products are so prolific that you can't say "something-a-chino" in a Starbucks these days without another aspiring writer opening a Mac laptop and continuing his or her work on the next great novel/screen-play/book of letters. (I should know. I've been in this Starbucks for 3 hours now and have seen at least 30 Macs open up.)

It seems, right now, that you are invincible. Billions of dollars in cash, a vast, profitable product line and a rock star reputation for releasing new products that create such "buzz" that a swarm of bees would, by comparison, seem like a lonely elderly housefly.

Which is why I'm very nervous about you guys.

I'm nervous that it will all come crashing down soon when some other upstart (which is what you were when you released your first comput-er) sneaks up on you and deems your products irrelevant. Sort of like you did with the PC computers that ran on Microsoft or, a little closer to home here in Canada, what your smartphone did to our formerly smarter phone, the BlackBerry.

Already it seems you and Samsung are involved in litigious battles every week, if not every day, about your competing patents and trademarks. Which is worrisome because apparently some of the parts IN your smartphones are made by Samsung. That's not the greatest way to keep a good relationship with your parts supplier, is it? Suing their virtual asses off? How can you do that and think they won't do something to retaliate? Something like creating microscopic Trojan horse–like components that will get inside your phones and destroy them like technical termites or nano–Nicki Minajes.

I'm not just saying this as a consumer, Apple. I also own some of your stock (as does, approximately, every other investor who is currently investing). It seems improbable, maybe even impossible, that your stock would suddenly crash. But it seemed that way with all the dotcom start-ups a while back too. As well as other massive companies whose ride to the top suddenly crashed to the bottom, taking little shareholders' life savings along with them.

So I guess what I'm saying here, Apple, is please keep up the good work! Please keep people at the top who won't drag you to the bottom. Please keep innovating and invigorating consumer technology. Don't IGNORE your competition. And please don't do anything stupid like developing a computer watch...

Uh-oh...I think it's time to diversify my portfolio a little bit.

Yours truly,
Steve Patterson
Apple Shareholder number 1,356,789,432,999,765.3

Dear squirrels,

I don't care what some people say. I quite like you crazy, death-defying little buggers.

With your ability to leap from branch to branch, tree to tree and even twig to nothing in particular, you're like the Cirque du Soleil of animals, only I don't have to pay to watch you.

You're right there in my backyard and up in the trees on my property, exclusively, it seems, for my entertainment.

Sure, there are some behavioural issues, such as when you treat flowers and seeds my wife has just planted like your own ALL-U-CAN-EAT buffet. Or when you engage in the squirrel-and-the-squirrel version of "the birds and the bees" right in front of my baby daughter's eyes. (Couldn't you at least go INSIDE the tree for that? Then it would only be as creepy as hearing people having sex in the next hotel room.) I also know you tend to drive dogs crazy by darting around them, just beyond their reach, like the most irritating of National Hockey League "pests" who draw penalties with cheap shots and verbal insults but will never drop the gloves themselves (I'm talking to you, Brad Marchand).

But for the most part, having you scamper around my backyard is a great way to start the day. You're like household pets that I don't have to feed, clean up after, pay vet bills for or touch.

So thanks, squirrels, you crazy nuts. And by all means, help yourself to that bird food. They can FLY somewhere else to get it. If you can crawl up that tiny pole and into that tiny little feeder, or kamikaze dive to it from the third-storey window, well, you deserve it.

Yours truly,
Steve Patterson
Man of the squirrels

Dear transport truck drivers,

First and foremost, I want to extend my thanks for the often thankless work that you do.

Transporting goods in a large transport truck is not an easy job. You drive thousands of miles, for thousands of hours, in a vehicle that weighs tens of thousands of pounds. For this you are paid many thousands of dollars, sure, but that schedule, most of which you spend sitting behind the wheel, means that some of you also weigh close to a thousand pounds yourselves. All of this so that drivers of comparatively tiny vehicles and comparatively tiny weights will have things to consume such as cars, Coca-Cola and "fresh" fruits and vegetables.

Along the way you have to deal with inclement weather, lengthy traffic delays and probably border and customs people who, in my comparatively few experiences of crossing the border in a car, can range from "pleasant enough" to "downright pricks."

This said, there is one small favour I would like to ask all of you.

When you are driving on the highway and come upon a slower truck in the right lane, could you kindly NOT PULL INTO THE PASSING LANE IN FRONT OF ME AND PROCEED TO TAKE A CALENDAR MONTH TO PASS?

This happens to me with shocking regularity. So much so, in fact, that I'm starting to think you guys do it ON PURPOSE. As if driving for hours and hours on end is so boring that the act of cutting off cars and watching the ensuing miles-long lineup form behind you gives you some sort of sadistic thri —

You know what? Forget it. If I had to drive in traffic as much as you guys do, filled with arsehole drivers (usually in luxury cars), I would do whatever I could to entertain myself too.

But if you wouldn't mind, AFTER you have cut me off in the passing lane and delayed my trip from anywhere between 3 minutes and 30 days, could you at least kindly honk your horn when I ask for it with the traditional pull-down motion that most of us learned as children but precious few of us still do as adults?

Much obliged, and keep on truckin'!

Yours truly,
Steve Patterson
Man in FORD trying to ESCAPE traffic

Dear local Member of Parliament,

I'm addressing you as such as a sign of respect (and because I have no idea what your name is).

Anyway, I'm writing in support of the recent public movement to legalize marijuana and to make a personal plea for you to subsidize it. Not for mere recreational use, of course, but for specific medicinal purposes.

Now I am not, technically speaking, "sick." But I was at a party recently where some second-hand marijuana smoke somehow got accidentally passed into my system...4 or 5 times...and you know what? It made me feel a lot better.

So that got me thinking. Maybe I <u>AM</u> sick and as such am entitled to government-subsidized marijuana.

Ipso facto, if I provide you with a "doctor's note" saying that I'm "sick," then this should act as a perfectly legal IOU to my dealer...sorry... "health-care provider," who will then take this to your office for reimbursement. Right?

I do understand that this is not the main purpose behind government involvement in the marijuana trade. You simply want to help those who are truly suffering with access to safe, pain-reducing marijuana. It has nothing to do with the billions of dollars in tax revenue it is expected to generate within a few short years. I wouldn't insult you by insinuating that was the reason you are considering this move.

So how about helping out a guy who pays his "fair share" of taxes and would now like to inhale his "fair share" of legal marijuana?

If you could get back to me ASAP, that would be greatly appreciated as my "health-care provider" is standing by as we speak with a sizable bag of soon-to-be law-abiding citizenship.

Respectfully yours,
Steve Patterson
Law-abiding citizen

Dear *Bachelor* and *Bachelorette*,

Just to be clear, this letter is to the reality shows *The Bachelor* and *The Bachelorette*, not simply all males and females who are not yet married. I'm sure many in those 2 groups are fine, productive people.

But the contestants on these shows are not.

I know I probably shouldn't single you guys out since there are many different reality shows whose participants I find equally pointless. But I thought you, of all people, would enjoy being "singled out."

Now, full disclosure (it's a legal term meaning "I probably shouldn't be saying this"): I have never watched a full episode of your shows. Just enough to realize that I didn't need to watch anymore. Which was about 37 seconds on 3 different occasions. Why did I go back 2 additional times? Because my wife watches you. Which I try not to make fun of her for because she categorizes you as a "guilty pleasure."

I categorize you as horseshi — sorry, I'll try to keep this classy — equine manure.

Why?

Because you have taken the concept of people "falling in love" and transmogrified it into a long, tedious, crying and make-out session that, now that I write this and read it out loud, seems a pretty accurate reflection of the process of "falling in love." On paper.

But in reality, nothing could be further from reality.

On your shows, one man or woman and several of the opposite gender are whisked around the world with host Chris Harrison (who shows up approximately 13 seconds of every episode and says "You know what to do" and then goes back to enjoying himself in exotic locales). Then, based on meaningless conversations and kissing, several women or men are sent home weekly until the one "true love" is revealed.

In reality, a man who is simultaneously dating even 2, let alone SEVERAL women who have ended up on the same remote island with him would not escape said island with either of his testicles intact.

Women or men who find out they are all dating the same person at the same time would instead devise a plan to make that person's life a living hell. Insults would ignite. Fists would fly. Social media campaigns would go viral, describing a sexually transmitted virus that may or may not actually exist (so at least the term "viral" would actually be in proper context for once). Meanwhile, deciding which of the many people you are simultaneously dating would receive a rose, as meaningful as a discarded banana peel, would be the least of that person's worries. In real life, each of those sweet-smelling roses would soon become a thorny suppository.

If THAT were how each episode of your shows ended, I think you'd be surprised how many more people might watch. Because for every vacuous person who has found true love with a beautiful idiot after directly competing for that idiot's affection with 24 other vacuous people, there are at least 20 real people who would give anything to stick a thorny rose up an arsehole's arse.

Yours truly,
Steve Patterson

PS: If my wife is reading this, I know you think watching the same set of sports highlights several times in a row is as "silly" as I think watching *The Bachelor* is. So let's call this one a draw.

Dear letter C,

I'm not sure what to make of you.

From a scholastic standpoint you are obviously subpar, being as you are the mark that the slackest of slacker students strive for as the pinnacle of achievement. (Even though you are often the correct choice on multiple-choice exams.)

In terms of pronunciation you are a bit of a chameleon, sometimes making a hard "ka" sound (as in the word "chameleon") and sometimes being soft, as in the word "ice." So what are you, C? Hard or soft? (Let's not make a puerile penis reference here, letter C. That's something I would do.)

Often you are the precursor of the letter H, as in "chug" or "chafe." Sometimes you are the precursor for the letter H twice in one word, as in "church."

When one thinks of "the C-word," one's thoughts often land in unpleasant territory.

But C can also be the mark of a strong leader. In hockey, a C on the front of the jersey indicates the captain. In business the CEO is the Chief (though many CEOs are also SOBs, but that's the topic of another letter).

C is for Country. C is for my country, Canada. Perhaps most importantly, C is for Cookie (that's good enough for me). These are all powerful things that bring people together. Especially Chocolate Chip Cookies, the best possible triple alliteration that starts with your appropriately crescent-shaped countenance.

But you are also cursed (another bad one) with being the beginning of one of the world's very worst words by all accounts: "cancer." It's a combo hard C–soft C that is as foreboding as it is confusing. No one likes that word. It's probably the reason a lot of people might understandably hate you. And really the only chance you have at removing that hatred is if one of the most powerful words that you also happen to be at the start of is found: a cure. That's really the best C word there is. So here's hoping for much more of the latter from you and the outright end to the former in the very near future.

Yours truly,
Steve Patterson

PS: I forgot to point out that you are also a homonym for the word that is the synonym for "body of salt water." But I figured that might confuse readers, so I didn't. Until now. Good talk.

Dear Satan (a.k.a. the Devil, Beelzebub, Lord of the Flies, Vladimir Putin),

I'm not sure exactly what to call you, and frankly it doesn't matter because I'm not going to call you. I can't believe I'm even writing you. But since reading long letters these days is considered "hellishly tedious," I thought I would give it a shot.

Anyway, just in case you were wondering, yes, you're an arsehole.

I understand that you believe your purpose is to exact evil on all living things, and — credit where credit is due — sometimes that's a good thing. Like when a drunken, moronic motorist runs into a tree, or when a cast member from *Jersey Shore* gets a nasty sunburn. Those are good-evil things.

But the evil-evil stuff, that's just inexcusable. From mad gunmen who storm schools full of innocent children to the arseholes in the NRA who support their right to do that, to terrorist organizations such as ISIS, or Islamic State, if you will (let's be honest; they should just be called Association of Radical Shithead Oppressive Losers, or "ARSOL"), there's really no call for that.

Most people, given the opportunity of a time machine, would choose to go back in time and kill your universally accepted chief minion, Adolf Hitler, before he could wreak the unthinkable tragedy of the Holocaust. No argument there. But perhaps going back even further to find the genesis of you would be beneficial as well.

You are said to be a "fallen angel," someone who didn't get your way in heaven, so you started a rival company down south. This happens in the IT world all the time. But you really took it to the next level, didn't you? Defying the commandments. Recruiting evil-doers. Hiding "weapons of mass destruction" in Iraq so deviously that they were never, in fact, found.

You tricky devil!

Look, I'm sorry things didn't work out for you in heaven. We all experience dissatisfaction with our jobs from time to time. But you have more than proven your point at this point.

Your legion of arseholes (Type A's, as I refer to them) have had a "good" (actually very BAD) run. But don't you think it's about time you hung up the pitchfork? Called off the arseholes of the world? Better yet, called them down to join you, so you can all be arseholes to each other? Terrorists love fighting other terrorists, so why not have them do it in front of you, the way we watch professional sports? (And let's be perfectly honest: there are quite a few pro athletes who are ready to join you down there as well.) Let the lawyers who live up to the lawyer jokes litigate to their lack-of-heart's content down there. Get a Goldman Sachs office going. And of course, you can have all the world's Walmarts.

All I'm saying here, Satan, is ... there comes a time in everyone's life — yes, even in the lives of "immortals" — when it's time to settle down and reap the rewards of a life's work.

Why not you? Why not now? Why not gather your entire Kingdom of arseholes right in front of you and watch them duke it out for your own personal entertainment: abusive athletes, bastardly bankers, proroguing prime ministers ... you get the idea. Bring the worst of the worst down to you and leave the boring, peaceful, friendly types up here to play fun, non-concussive sports and engage in consensual sex.

As for those for whom that sounds like hell, well, you can also have them down there to show them the difference.

Thanks for your time.

> Respectfully not yours,
> Steve Patterson

Dear airlines,

Look, I know you get a lot of grief from a lot of people about a lot of things.

Such as "delayed flights" that, after hours, turn into "cancelled flights," or "lost luggage" or "luggage that went to a better destination than I did," or fees that are not just "extraordinary" but *extortionary*. (Not a word yet, but you know what I mean.)

This letter isn't about any of those things. This letter is about booking more people on a flight than you have seats for.

I'm not sure when this became an established industry practice, but I can tell you that no other industry I know of practices it. Music concerts generally sell exactly as many tickets as a venue has seats. (Unless it's general admission, which might have no seats at all, just people packed into a roped-off general area. But I don't want to give you guys any <u>more</u> weird ideas). Once the seats for a concert are sold out, they advertise that the show is "sold out." Or they add another show. They don't just assume that a certain percentage of people <u>won't show up </u>to the concert they bought tickets for. Or that some people won't mind strangers sitting on their laps. (Again, please don't get any ideas.) This is because the vast majority (100%) of people who pay for tickets to concerts by their favourite musical artists tend to <u>attend those concerts</u> and/or pass those tickets on to friends or sell them to others.

This isn't an option on airlines. Airline tickets are "non-transferable." Therefore, every person who buys a seat is the only person who can use that seat. And I would guess that most people who buy an airline ticket do so because they have a need or at the very least a strong desire to fly to a specific destination at a specific time.

This occurred to me on a recent flight that was "oversold," and "volunteers" were being offered "cash compensation and overnight accommodation" to give up their seats and fly out the next day. I'll be honest. I thought about it. But I had to get to a city to do a comedy show for a theatre full of people. And I wondered at that point whether anyone who was attending my show that night would be told, "Sorry, we're oversold, but we'll give you cash if you'll give up your seat and come back when Steve performs here again, maybe in 18 months."

Would my fans forgo the pleasure of my comedy that night for cash compensation?

I imagine they would, yes. Bad example.

Back to the topic at hand, how do you decide who gets "bumped" off a flight or offered compensation? Is it simply the last one to buy a ticket? Is there a complicated algorithm you use? Do you have a dartboard with all the passengers' photos on it and a monkey to toss darts at it? (Because if so, you should absolutely post that on YouTube.)

Furthermore, have you ever been faced with a situation where every passenger had an equally compelling (and logical) reason why they should be allowed on to the flight they booked a seat on, such as, "I want to get out of here because I don't live or work here, and if I don't get back to work on time, I won't live or work ANYWHERE!"

I imagine that has happened before. Many times. And your only choice is to give those people a job with your airline in that city. Which explains why so many of your counter staff are so counter-productive and indifferent to passengers — as illustrated by the hypothetical (but not all THAT hypothetical) conversation below:

> PASSENGER: "Please help me!"
>
> COUNTER STAFF: "There's nothing I can do."
>
> PASSENGER: "LET ME SPEAK TO YOUR MANAGER!"
>
> COUNTER STAFF: "I AM the manager. Have been since my flight was oversold 3 weeks ago."

If that's not how it works, I'm completely mystified how you guys continue doing this to the public or how the last airline manager I got into
an argument with could possibly have gotten that job.

Yours truly,
Steve Patterson
Airline manager-in-waiting

Dear Justin Bieber,

Look, young man, it would be easy to sit here and criticize all that you seem to have become: an obnoxiously rich, obnoxiously famous, obnoxiously obnoxious little shit who "represents" Canada wherever he goes.

But I'm not going to do that.

Given the level of wealth and fame you have accumulated at such a tender age (all as the result of busking in Stratford, Ontario, putting that video on YouTube and then that video being viewed by millions of people, including a grown man named "Scooter," who showed it to pop star Usher, who launched your celebrity career), it's really no surprise how irresponsibly you have acted when not on stage. Heck, I did some of the things you have done (bar fights, house-egging, getting arrested) when I was in my 20s with approximately one billionth of the fame and fortune.

But I, for one, am pulling for you to turn it back around and become a legitimate musical artist that your country and your mother can be proud of. (Your dad is proud of the delinquent you're being now, as evidenced by the fact he was just caught drag-racing WITH you in Miami.)

Like it or not, you're a role model now, Justin. Well, role models have responsibilities. The responsibility to inspire others to be the best people they can be. The responsibility to use their talent and resources to help those who deserve to be helped in the hope that they will "pay it forward" and help others when they are able.

You've got the power to do those things, young man, in a way that few, if any, Canadian artists have ever had before. No one can <u>force</u> you to be this way, of course. Ultimately no one can force YOU to do anything. Unless you are forced to go to jail by a judge for continued illegal behaviour, in which case other, much larger, much "badder" people with nothing to lose may force you to do a whole bunch of things you don't want to do.

So here's hoping you'll manage to find it within yourself to be an amazing role model. To make all of Canada and all of the world "Beliebe" in the positive power that you can share. I know it's a lot to ask, but it would be nice if, next time you are in the news, it was for something GOOD.

Yours truly,
Steve Patterson
Hopeful future Belieber

I wrote this upon learning that it is a tradition in the United States for the outgoing president to leave a letter of advice on the desk of the Oval Office for the incoming president. I thought to myself, "What would a letter from George W. Bush to Barack Obama look like?"

By the time you read this, President Obama's days in the White House will be dwindling or passed entirely, so I present this letter for historical purposes only. All spelling and punctuation mistakes here are intenshunal.

Dear 44!

43 here☺ Did you know my daddy was number 41? True story. That's what we call each other on special occasions. He says "Merry Christmas, 43!" and I say "Happy holidays, 41!" because that's the more potili.. plolili...that's the <u>right</u> way to say it.

Listen, you can go ahead and call me Dubya if you want as long as I can go ahead and call you B.O....Hey! I just realized your initials are B.O.! That's a bummer of a duogram buddy...

Anyway here's some advice for your new home here in the Oval Office. First thing you'll notice is...no corners!!! That's right, it's an oval. Turns out that's another word for circle. Did you know that? I didn't know that. Just found out when I used this new Microsoft Word dickshionary.

Second thing you'll notice is the desk. It was a gift from one of the Queens of England. Either Liz or Vicki...maybe Elton John, I don't know☺☺ But when you have a guest from England make sure you have that thing displayed pre-madonnaly. It looks like you could do a lot of important work on there...you know, if you're into that sort of thing.

Most importantly, though, you'll notice there are 2 thick, comfy sofas. Make sure you invite every guest to the Oval Office to lie down on those sofas. On a good day you'll make like 7 bucks in change! And given what I'm leaving you with, that could come in awful handy.

Well, that's about it, B.O. Everything else you'll pretty much learn as you go. Clinton can tell you about the secret entrances and exits, but I've seen your wife so you won't have much use for those. She is lovely. And scary. That's not a woman you cheat on!

I'd tell you more but that is honestly everything I've learned in the last 8 years here. So good luck. Take care. Stay black.

Dubya

PS: There was a message on the phone about some British oil company cutting some corners in the Gulf of Louisiana but I erased it. Probably nothin'. Good luck.

Dear sun-dried tomatoes,

Who the hell do you think you are?

Somehow you've established yourself as a "gourmet food delicacy," believing yourself to be superior to your everyday, off-the-vine tomatoes by virtue of... drying out in the sun?

Please.

If time spent drying out in the sun were truly a sign of superiority, then most people from California would be the finest humans in the world. Which, as anyone who follows TMZ knows, is simply not the case.

How is it that you, spending all your time drying out in the sun, have UPPED your stock?

Well, apparently, it's all in the salt.

I understand the process of making you involves covering normal tomatoes in salt and herbs and then... wait for it... *leaving them out in the sun to dry*, for between 4 days and 2 weeks. Which is impressive. Because humans left out in the hot sun that same amount of time, even with a sunscreen with an SPF of 400, would die of dehydration. Irish people like myself would, in fact, burst into flames within the first 4 minutes. So I suppose your ultra-longevity in ultra-violet rays is to be commended.

Or is it?

How is it that you have claimed the whole "sun-dried" industry while other fruits and/or vegetables (which one of these are you, anyway? — maybe I'll write another letter) haven't? Oranges are out in the California sunshine on trees for 7 to 12 MONTHS before they are ready to be picked off. Yet they are not referred to as "sun-dried" but simply "Sunkist." Who wants to be kissed for 7 to 12 months continuously (other than contestants on *The Bachelor*)?

"Sun-dried apples" are disgusting. Same for "sun-dried peaches." Sun-dried pears? Arguably worse than sun-dried peaches. Sun-dried grapes... Wait a minute. Those are just raisins! Not everyone knows this, because those rascally raisins chose a completely different name from how they began life. Like "Tom Cruise" (Thomas Cruise Mapother IV) or "Elton John" (Reginald Dwight) or "Engelbert Humperdinck" (that's right, he was born Arnold George Dorsey but CHOSE to change his name to ENGELBERT HUMPERDINCK because, I guess, Ezekiel Fartwheel was taken). But grapes decided "sun-dried grapes" wasn't appealing (or, I guess, a-peeling) enough. So they made up an entirely different name so no one would know what they were.

Well, that changes a lot.

You guys just say exactly what you are: tomatoes, left out in the sun for days on end, to dry.

You poor little bastards. You're like survivors of a shipwreck. Or *Sports Illustrated* swimsuit models. I guess the least we can do is consume you. I'm sorry about what I said at the start of this letter. I will put you on my next pizza, alongside some tomato sauce, which has met a similar fate to yours except it has been squeezed from a young ripe tomato, thrown into a can and then boiled alive... and then thrown in an oven.

Come to think of it, we humans really are dinks to you tomatoes, aren't we?

Sorry again,
Steve Patterson
Respect ALL tomatoes!

Dear letter T,

I like you. I like you a lot. Obviously not as much as Mr. T, who is such a big fan he changed his name to you, but I'm up there.

For one thing, I like your versatili...wait for it...T!

Not only are you a fine letter in fine words like, well, "letter," as well as being my favourite type of casual shirt, but you are also a word unto yourself: as in "tea": a drink with jam and bread. Or "tee": a tiny little pedestal for golf balls. Or the start of a giggle, as in "tee-hee-hee." Pretty much whenever you hear the term "T time," something that you enjoy is about to happen. A round of golf, a sipping of a caffeinated beverage... Heck, some even have "high tea," where elderly women dress up in fancy hats and put their tea-drinking GLOVES on and then apparently put something into their tea that is hallucinogenic. Sounds T-errific to me!

You are also one half of one of my favourite letter duos: T & A (though to be honest, I'm more of a T man myself).

But perhaps most importantly, you are the only letter that is a virtual time-travel machine. Partly because you lead off both the words "time" and "travel," but mostly because there is no other letter in the alphabet that can take you from "here" to "there."

That's all you, letter T.

I would call you "mister," but as we've already discussed, that name has officially been taken by a lovable '80s action star, and I think he really needs to hold on to it for now. Also, with your versatili...T (sorry, last time, I promise) when it comes to casual caffeinated beverages, casual shirts, giggly laughter and putting up with tiny, dimpled balls, I'm almost sure you are a woman, and a lovely one at that.

Yours truly,
Steve Patterson

PS: I just realized you are also featured more than any other letter in my name (except for E, but that arsehole is in EVERY word more than any other letter). That's 3 times as often as you appear in Mr. T's name, as a matter of fact. So maybe I AM your biggest fan.

Dear Australians,

G'day, mates.

I just want to say, on behalf of any Canadians who have ever met any of you, thanks for being our cool, crazy, cousins on the other side of the world.

From your love of sport to your love of barbeque to having beers that the rest of the world THINKS you guys drink but very few of you actually do (hello, FOSTER'S and Labatt's Blue), you lads and ladies really are more like us "Canucks" than any other nationality I've ever interacted with. (Sorry to my American friends, but it's true.)

For one thing, you're a contrarian bunch that still finds a way to be included in the Queen's Commonwealth. That's not easy. Other members of the British Empire have had British values imposed upon them to the point where they've lost their own identity. Not us. Sure, we're happy to have princes and princesses visit, and we still have the Queen on some of our money, and our old people still watch *Coronation Street*. But we have our own laws, our own way of life and even our own languages.

Where we end sentences with "eh" —as in "Great day, eh?" — you end sentences with "no worries" — as in "Just got in a fight with a shark... no worries."

And that points to the one major difference I have observed between you and us. You guys are, and I mean this in the best way possible, a little bit CRAZIER.

I observed this while aboard my favourite oxymoron in Sydney, the "Manly Ferry," a large ferry boat that criss-crosses Sydney Harbour from... wait for it... Manly. On this day the weather was rough and our large boat was rocking badly from side to side. But I seemed to be the only one remotely nervous about it. Everyone else aboard, seemingly Australian (judging from their Australian accents) sat calmly reading or talking, basically emanating "no worries" while I sat thinking, "So this is where it all ends, eh?"

Then I looked out the window during one of the giant rolls from side to side and saw that there was a man in the middle of the harbour, WINDSURFING.

To be fair, there are some Canadians who would do the same thing. Just not as many, I don't think. As evidenced by the fact that I learned to snowboard in Banff from an Australian lad who had crossed the world to teach Canadians how to ski. That's ballsy. Sort of like a Canadian going to Sydney to teach Australians how to surf.

Other than that, though, and the fact that you guys tan better than us, I believe our 2 "Commonwealth" countries are uncommonly alike. Which is why I look forward to bringing my family back over to your country to see you beautifully crazy people again as soon as possible.

Yours truly,
Steve Patterson
Aussie Aussie Aussie. Oi Oi Oi.

Dear flowers,

I'm not sure whether to express my sincere gratitude on behalf of all men who have ever screwed up or my sincere apologies on behalf of all humans who have severed you off at the shins to make a table pretty.

So I'll do both.

First of all, thanks very much from us men who have used you to make a good first impression on a potential mate and/or a good first step out of the proverbial "doghouse."

I remember buying my high-school girlfriend 17 roses 17 days before her 17th birthday, and let's just say, that move kept that girlfriend with me right through until prom (at which point I screwed up the relationship forever, but still, thanks!). I'm not sure when the time-honoured tradition of men buying flowers for women began, but I imagine it was in the Cro-Magnon era, when cave boy Thorg Jr. decided to show cave girl Gluglu his affection by ripping some pretty plants out of the ground and gently placing them in her hands rather than clubbing her unconscious with a tree branch.

Then, once Gluglu shared her story with her cave girl friends, Thorg Jr.'s dad (Thorg) realized that if he ever wanted the chance to make a sibling for Jr. he would have to make up for having clubbed Mrs. Thorg (there were no surnames in the Cro-Magnon era) on the head in the first place. So he pulled some plants out of the ground, blew on some sand until it turned into a glass shape he called a "vase" and gave that to Mrs. Thorg. Miraculously, it worked. So he did it again whenever he arrived back to the cave a little later than expected (even if he had genuinely been "wrestling a woolly mammoth" the entire time, just as he told her).

Ever since then, men have shown their genuine love/remorse/condolences with flowers. Which is beautiful. So...thank you for that.

This said, I'm really sorry that we chose to do this by cutting you off at the knees (do you have knees?), choking you from your water source, hacking away at your dismembered stem until it suits the shape we're looking for and then, after about a week's time, throwing out your limp, lifeless body in the garbage. When put in this context, we really should be compensating YOU with a gift for truly unacceptable behaviour. So...do you have any friends you'd like me to chop down and bring you?

Yours truly,
Steve Patterson
Frequent flower-bringer

Dear fire,

As I write this, you are burning through large swaths of forest in Saskatchewan and British Columbia as well as California and I'm sure many other places around the planet that I don't know of. Some say this is a seasonal thing, exaggerated by current drought conditions, while others say it is the beginning of the end of the world, brought on by human-initiated climate change.

I'm hoping that those "others" are wrong.

But I figured I might as well ask you directly, since there is no real reason for you to lie to me: If you are indeed intent on burning your way through planet Earth right now, please do NOT do that.

Why not (you ask in a fiery voice somewhere between Sam Elliott and Marilyn Manson)?

Well, first of all Earth's surface is something like 70% water (it might be higher and/or lower; I didn't pay a lot of attention during geography class), so even if you burn everything you can, that's only 30%. The only other thing that finds fulfillment at that level of success is major league baseball batters.

Second of all, humans and fire work so much better together than against each other. Remember that steak you and I cooked last night? It was perfect. Seared on the outside, pink in the middle, delicious. I couldn't have done that without you. And surely you must have enjoyed the juices that fell through the grill. There's also the age-old "campfire," where humans of varying degrees of musical and storytelling ability gather around for impromptu performances. Granted, much of the singing is off-key, some of the stories are terrible, and after an evening's steady flow of Irish whisky, there's a good chance that whisky will flow again in the form of a man peeing into you. But still it has a magical quality to it. Besides, how many marshmallows have we given you over the years when they fell off sticks? That pretty much evens out the whole peeing-on-you thing, doesn't it?

There's also the lighting of torches for nighttime illumination (also the Olympics…and angry mobs), the cauterizing of wounds, the smithing of swords, the blowing of glass and glorious fireworks that delight holiday revellers while simultaneously culling a handful of idiots from the human herd.

Maybe most importantly, you hold the power to turn any cake, even a cupcake, into a <u>birthday</u> cake. I know of no better magical power.

We are capable of great things together, fire. But not if you keep burning down our forests with your selfish, resource-sucking, gluttonous ways. Even if it's OUR selfish, resource-sucking, gluttonous ways that gave you the idea.

So what do you say, my fiery friend? Can we at least sit down and talk this out over a joint? I know you've got a light.

Yours truly,
Steve Patterson
Friend of flames when the flames are friendly

Dear investment advisors,

It can't be easy doing what you do.

On the one hand, just having to sit all day watching and analyzing numbers the rest of us avoid like the plague is difficult enough.

But to then have to explain those numbers to us non-advisors, many of whom still think "RESP" is just the beginning of Aretha Franklin's most famous tune, well, that must be like explaining theoretical physics to a contestant on *The Bachelorette*.

On top of that, while I'm sure there are many more good people in your industry than bad, it is the bad ones who make the news and so infuriate the public with schemes robbing people's life savings that your industry may actually be more reviled than any other, except maybe parking police. (Note to self: Write a letter to parking police.)

My advisor is a lovely, patient woman named Julie who sets aside good chunks of time for me whenever I need it to go over my portfolio. She does this partly because she is a wise professional and a caring teacher and mostly because I pay her a good chunk of my portfolio to make sure it keeps growing.

What I like about Julie is that she knows exactly how much risk I am comfortable with. I am what your industry officially refers to as a "moderate risk" client. Meaning I understand that if you want reward (i.e., growing money), you will have to endure some risk (i.e., dastardly downturns). Plus I have some time for this money to grow (I hope). But I am not a "high risk" client, in that if I see my portfolio dip by 10% or more, there is a "high risk" of my having a heart attack.

I won't get into the specifics of it (because I really don't fully understand them), but my portfolio has grown nicely over the past few years. I know exactly how much I have paid in fees, and when I watch the news I've never seen Julie being led away from her office in handcuffs. That's enough for me.

Which leads me to the reason I'm writing this letter. I think your industry, more than any other, is guilty of putting out too much information (TMI).

When individuals use this expression, it usually refers to the over-sharing of personal information, as in, "My doctor says the rash might be contagious," or "What do you think of this photo of my genitals?"

But in your industry, it simply means there is too much coming at us at all times. There are stock exchange tickers on information channels, instant stock updates on smartphones, annual reports from each company within a 100-company mutual fund and my personal nemesis, the "simplified prospectus." These things arrive in my mailbox every 3 months, and I immediately transfer them to the recycling bin, still in their original packaging (a trick my childhood friend taught me with hockey trading cards, so they don't lose value).

The "simplified prospectus" is a collection of information in print so small it couldn't be read with the world's most powerful microscope. If I actually took the time to read the entire prospectus (which I did once, like an idiot), I finished with a migraine headache and a feeling of confusion I hadn't experienced since I mistakenly watched half of a David Cronenberg film.

I've spoken to quite a few fellow investors, and it seems we all universally not only do not read these prospectuseseses (prospecti?), but we all treat them as if they are used diapers, from children other than our own, that we are forced to dispose of.

So here is what I am suggesting to you...

Ideally, STOP SENDING ANNUAL REPORTS AND "SIMPLIFIED PROSPECTUSES." The information I want, I go get online. We may save a large forest's worth of paper. And let's face it, paper stocks could use the boost.

Most importantly, if you are going to call something "simplified," then actually make it simple. Like a children's book. With smiley faces where your portfolio has gone UP, frowny faces where your portfolio has gone down, CLEARLY STATED figures of how much your portfolio has gone up or down, and whether or not the whereabouts of your investment advisor are still known.

That's all you need to send. That's all we want to read. That's all I have to say. Good talk.

Yours truly,
Steve Patterson
Moderate investor

Dear Ireland,

I miss you. I miss you a lot.

Not that I am technically "from" you. Going back a few generations in my family, there is some Irish lineage. But the same can be said of President Obama. And though his name sounds pretty Irish (but not as Irish as it would if it were O'Bama), both he and I are about as genuinely Irish as Kenny Rogers's current face is "the original."

However, having travelled to Ireland many times and performed there, I really do feel like I'm at home when I am in you. (Grow up.)

Perhaps it's the pub lifestyle. Sitting in an authentic Irish pub, talking to people you've just met like they're old friends while live music plays in the corner, is one of my favourite ways to spend an afternoon. There's no place better to do this than in Ireland. (No matter how "authentic" an Irish pub somewhere else claims to be, it's not as authentic as an authentic pub in Ireland.)

But I have gone out into your fine countryside as well, and the air in Ireland is fresher than anywhere else I've ever experienced. This despite the disservice that Irish Spring soap has done to your air's reputation over the years.

From Dublin's bustling Grafton Street in the Temple Bar district to the Cliffs of Moher on your west coast, for me there's no country so easy to get across and hard to resist getting back to. I even love the way Irish people give directions, like saying that Dublin is "10 minutes" from Galway (it's about 3 hours by train) or that the roads will "rise to meet you," a much more pleasant way of saying, "You'll probably fall down drunk on the way home from the pub."

Even Belfast in Northern Ireland, which I know is under "British rule" (but you and I both know it belongs to you), is a charming place that despite its troubled history of "the Troubles" is a thriving destination for university students, tourists and travelling comedians alike. Matter of fact, I liked Belfast so much the last time I was there that I missed a train back to Dublin the next day thanks to the hospitality of some locals who used "that funny Canadian fella" as an excuse for a Tuesday night party that went well into Wednesday.

And that's the REAL best part and best export of Ireland: real Irish people. There is simply no more hospitable group on Earth than them (except perhaps Canadian Maritimers, but a lot of them came from Ireland, so they're technically still YOU). Through the famine and the Troubles and that crazy snake epidemic that St. Patrick had to rid you of (topic of another letter in this book), the Irish people have kept their eyes smilin', their voices singin' and their love of life shinin' from within. Which is good because if there is one thing the Irish CAN'T do, it's tan properly.

I hope to be back soon, Ireland. Start that Guinness for me now, please.

Sláinte,
Steve Patterson

Dear perfume commercial creators,

Maybe I'm not your target market in that I don't wear perfume, but who, exactly, IS your target market?

From what I've seen, it seems to be people on hallucinogenic drugs who enjoy bizarre dream sequences.

Your common elements include:

- a fit, handsome man in a swimsuit diving into water

- a fit, beautiful woman, also in a swimsuit and often with giant bird wings and a "come hither" expression (as if a man who encountered a bird-woman wouldn't be terrified)

- actual birds flying away (the most sensible living things IN the commercial)

- a passionate mock-make-out session on a beach

- the reveal of the perfume's ridiculous name, such as Eternity (if the scene depicted here were anyone's eternity, it would be a terrifying existence of unending sexual frustration) or Chanel No. 5 (this is the best you could come up with after 5 TRIES?)

I get that you need to create something opulent, given the money you want people to pay for a few ounces of stink water. But honestly, does anyone see these things and then immediately head to the store, saying,

"QUICK! GIVE ME SOME OF THAT STUFF THAT MAKES YOUNG MEN DIVE AT ME AND WINGS GROW FROM MY BACK!"

"Do you remember the name of it, ma'am?"

"Um...I think it was Enter Me?"

I'm not a marketing expert, but I think it might be a better idea, given that women who purchase perfume are trying to cover up their natural scent, to depict the scene of what WOULD happen if they didn't wear it as opposed to what will NOT happen if they do.

Example: A woman walks into a bar full of men. Sadly, she has no wings attached. She approaches a man who is standing, fully dressed (rather than a man who is diving into water and therefore probably doesn't want to be APPROACHED). The man sniffs at the air, turns up his nose and walks away. The woman yells angrily for the other men to hear: "OH YEAH? WELL YOU DON'T EXACTLY SMELL LIKE A ROSE YOURSELF, BUDDY! NONE OF YOU DO!" Then she storms out. Finally, the name of the perfume is revealed: « Couvrez votre puanteur » ("Cover your stink").

Will it fulfill a fantasy? No. Will it sell your product? Probably not. But it sure as hell makes more sense. And it gives far more credit to consumers' sense of humour than your current crop of crap.

Yours truly,
Steve Patterson
Former full-time ad copywriter. Go figure.

Dear Bigfoot,

I'm not sure if this letter will ever reach you because I'm not really sure you exist. But if you do and it does, you should know this: people are looking for you.

A lot of people. And they're not just "looking." They're actually HUNTING. I learned this from watching something on the internet called "Hunting Bigfoot," where several men, armed mostly with sound equipment, were off in the woods somewhere talking about you.

They hadn't actually ever seen you before. (I always find this is a tough challenge for a hunter. Because if you don't know what the thing you are hunting looks like, how do you know if you see it?) But they had a very grainy video of "you" they were working from. It's actually called "the Patterson film" because it was shot by a guy named Roger Patterson (no relation).

I'm not sure if you knew you were the star of a film. It makes sense if you didn't since no one is really sure it's you. I've watched it a few times now, and honestly it could just be an Italian man looking for dropped metal on the beach.

But in case you did go for a stroll one day in 1967 and then wondered, "Did anyone get any grainy footage of that?" well, the answer is... maybe.

As long as I've got you, I just have a couple of quick questions.

First off, is there a Mrs. Bigfoot? I'm not asking for me. I'm happily married. Just wondering if there's someone out there for you to spend time with and/or who hasn't let you leave the house for the past 47 years or so.

Second, what do you eat? I'm guessing you're a carnivore, judging from your frame in the video. Also, it looks like you're not a stranger to beer (probably Kokanee, if beer commercials are accurate). But what if you're a vegetarian? Maybe even a vegan? Maybe you're allergic to gluten, which means you're probably dead now because this allergy only cropped up a little while back, and if you haven't been eating gluten-free…well, sorry, big guy. Or big girl…

That brings me to my last question. Are you, maybe, a female? Again, with only one video to judge from, it's tough to tell because your back is to the camera. I'm not a pervert and I wouldn't want to pry, but are you a lady? If so, in the event you are ever found, you're going to want to go straight to a spa for a mani-pedi. And I'm going to suggest some serious waxing too. It will hurt a bit, but from what I'm told, it's worth it. Even if you are a male, it's still a good idea. Something called "manscaping." Helps improve your swimming speed too.

Anyway, Mr. or Mrs. Foot, thanks for taking the time to read this, and congratulations on evading those who have been hunting you for over 4 decades now. If nothing else, you are very, very good at hide-and-seek and should perhaps consider working as a sales associate at The Bay.

Yours truly,
Steve Patterson
Medium-sized feet

Dear pinky toenails,

Have you ever wondered why you exist?

I guess all of us do at one point or another, and it's an existential question that can lead to a myriad of complicated answers philosophically. But in your case I mean it LITERALLY: why do human bodies need pinky toenails?

Maybe it's different for people who wear toenail polish.

If you paint your other toes and NOT your pinky toe, it's simply unfair. Like giving 4 children birthday presents but not the tiny, inconsequential fifth child. (Full disclosure: I'm the youngest of 5 children.)

But for those of us who don't wear toenail polish intentionally (there have been a couple of parties I've passed out at, plus I have several nieces), the pinky toenail seems more useless than the appendix. Indeed, you only notice you have an appendix when it needs to be surgically removed. Few if any people have ever gone in to the hospital for an emergency "pinky-toenail-a-dectomy." But if they did and they came out sans pinky toenail, I'm sure no one including them would notice the difference.

I say all this realizing it may come off as mean. Maybe you do indeed fulfill a purpose, such as protecting the skin underneath you from the sun or tiny pebbles when walking in flip-flops or when under attack from Lilliputians like in *Gulliver's Travels* (those sneaky little bastards would for sure try to infiltrate the human body through the pinky toe).

Or maybe you are there so that extremely flexible people such as yoga experts have something to look at when they bring their foot up across their face and into their eyeball.

Or maybe you are just there to remind us that everything plays a part in the miracle of life. Every little part of every person's body. Even the ones that are so small and grow so slowly and are so difficult to handle that you wonder why you even bother with them in the first place. It's about RESPECT. Pay loving attention to the smallest detail and it is infinitely better for the whole...

Whoa.

That's pretty deep, pinky toe. This has been a good talk. See you again next time my toenails need cutting.

Yours truly,
Steve Patterson
Owner of adorable, wise, twin pinky toenails

Dear political polling companies,

Beyond the statistics, percentages and data gathering methods that you use, I have just one question: how is it that you are allowed to still be in business when you are so often SO wrong?

Recent examples include BC premier Christy Clark winning a majority for the Liberals in BC, despite trailing rivals by 20% in several polls leading up to the election. Meanwhile, and certainly bigger as mistakes go, a guy on FOX News named Dick Morris assured viewers that Mitt Romney would defeat Barack Obama in a "landslide" in 2012 using the following formula:

> We are taking 4 elections — '04, '06, '08 and '10, and we are averaging them, and then we're weighting the data according to that average. And when you do that?... Romney will win this election by 5 to 10 points in the popular vote and will carry more than 300 electoral votes.

How wrong was Dick? Well, no one calls Mr. Romney Mr. President now, do they? I'm not even sure they call him Mr. Romney. They probably just call him Mitt and then giggle out loud.

Around the world, polling companies continue to poll, <u>decisions continue to be made based on your projections,</u> and your projections continue to be wildly wrong.

Of course, you never explicitly predict election outcomes (unless you're a Dick Morris). You always give a disclaimer such as, "These predictions are considered correct 19 times out of 20, + or − 3%," which is another way of saying, "There's a pretty good chance these predictions are wrong."

If you're interested in knowing why your projections are often so far off, I can tell you why: people are not machines. People change their minds. People forget to go vote or sometimes don't vote on purpose. Maybe most importantly, <u>people lie.</u>

Sort of like if Jesus Himself called you up and asked if you were going to go to church this coming Sunday. About 99.9% of respondents would say, "Yes, absolutely, I will, Jesus!" While 0.1% would be justifiably skeptical that Jesus would be calling them on the phone. Yet come Sunday, you might see only 9% of those respondents actually at church.

If respondents would hypothetically lie to Jesus, they will absolutely lie to you pollsters.

You also underestimate human hunger and appetite, which is the only way to explain calling people at dinnertime. Even those who want to be good citizens and/or are too polite to hang up, desperately want to eat that delicious-smelling food on their plate. How can this not affect their answers?

> "Who will you be voting for in the coming election?"

> "Brisket with a Dijon rub."

> "Excuse me?"

> "Oh, sorry. Who's running again?"

> "Well there's Stephen Har — "

> "Never mind. Just put me down for whoever's name is closest to Brisket. OK?" (Takes bite of brisket. Moans with pleasure.)

> "Um…OK. Thanks for your time."

> (Mumbling through.) "Mmmmmm. Bye."

I stand by this statement 100% of the time, 20 times out of 20. Put that in your poll and smoke it.

> Yours truly,
> Steve Patterson
> Or, as pollsters know me:

"Dr. Maria Alvarez
24-year-old female
Conservative supporter
$7 trillion annual income
Big fan of Nickelback"

Dear letter D,

I don't really have much to say to you because, to be honest, I don't think of you very much.

It could be because you are a grade in school that I'm not sure even exists. I mean once you've earned less than a C, you might as well just put F, right? Anyone who gets a D knows that they actually failed.

Or it might just be because the Detroit Tigers baseball team chose, as their logo, the calligraphy version of you, which has never made sense to me. I'm pretty sure a tiger couldn't hold a pen well enough with its ungainly paws to make the mark of even a preschooler's cursive D, let alone an ornate calligraphic version. What kind of tiger would take the time to learn that? Tigers don't need calligraphy as their calling card. If a tiger wants your attention, it will either maul you to death or tell you you're "grrrrrrrrreat!" and THEN slowly kill you with a sugary breakfast you have been led to believe was nutritious.

On the bright side, though, with the simple act of doubling yourself, everything changes. Good old "double down" promises a chance of twice the winnings (and also twice the losings, but I'm trying to be positive here), and simply stating "DOUBLE D" puts a smile on my face almost as large as the visual it conjures. It brings me back to an ex-girlfriend who had a huge...smile and a larger-than-life personality.

Good memories indeed. Good old Double D (her name was Diana Davis).

So, you've got that going for you, D. Two of you are indeed much better than one.

Yours truly,
Steve Patterson

PS: Actually, Double D wasn't named Diana Davis. Her name was Michelle. She just had really big boobs.

Dear onions,

I'll be honest here… The only reason I am writing this is for the opportunity to make YOU cry for a change. Which I realize is unlikely, given your lack of tear ducts or emotions.

But on behalf of everyone who has been forced to explain why they are bawling their eyes out when all they were trying to do was prepare a meal, I think it's worth a shot.

So — first things first — what's it like being the poster vegetable for halitosis (that's a big word for "bad breath," you stupid orb). Sure, garlic is bad too. And coffee gets some play. But coffee is essential for many people to start their day. Garlic is used to protect human souls from blood-sucking vampires. You are neither an essential day-starter nor a potential soul-saver. So really, all you do is give us bad breath. Way to go, onions. (That was sarcasm, which you probably don't understand because you're a dumb onion.)

Next, what's with all the layers? What are you trying to hide? Other vegetables have one outer layer, which is relatively easy to cut through and gives way to the "good part" of the vegetable inside. Like carrots. Or potatoes. Many veggies don't even have an outer layer to fight through, like broccoli or celery. They hide nothing. Why should they? They don't give people bad breath.

You onions are a multi-layered fortress of deception, with an outer layer made up of some sort of semi-malleable membrane that must be cut AND peeled, revealing ring after ring of tear gas. And those are the "good onions." The more deceitful ones — my nemesis, "red onions" — are so inherently dishonest that they are actually coloured PURPLE. Why call yourself one thing when you are another? Because you are a con artist, that's why. You're a con artist and nobody likes you, and that's why we keep cutting you up into tiny pieces and discarding your skin into compost where even raccoons won't eat you, and they will eat literally EVERYTHING ELSE. But not you, because you'll give them breath more horrible than eating garbage. <u>SO SUCK ON THAT,</u> <u>ONIONS</u>…

Doesn't feel very good, does it?

Maybe that was a little too far.

Sorry if I made you cry…but you started it!

    Yours truly,
    Steve Patterson

PS: You do smell delicious when frying, though.

Dear "gluten" (if that is your real name),

I have a few questions for you, if you don't mind:

1. What are you?

2. Why are so many people allergic to you?

3. Why is it sooooo irritating when someone says they are allergic to you?

I know I could probably just Google you and find out, but that seems impersonal, so I'd rather ask you directly, you know, man to...whatever it is you are.

I do have a working theory.

Considering that you were not in existence during my childhood or adolescence, I have deduced that you appeared around 1990, presumably from outer space, targeting people who like to eat but much prefer to WORRY. Your reputation preceded you, so that when you arrived (via space shuttle to Houston), people were already terrified.

"There's a new allergy out there, folks," I can almost hear a Texan doctor saying from beneath a giant cowboy hat, "and it's called GLUTEN!" Then a woman screamed, dogs cowered and parents of Earth-children raced to their local hospitals.

"Help us!" they implored. "My little boy has the gluten!"

Children were quarantined. Towns were evacuated. Nutritionists appeared on the evening news, referred to for the first time in their existence as "experts."

Studies were conducted. Scientists determined that you had come from space to attack humans via the arse muscles (a.k.a. the "glutes") and that any human who didn't want to have their arse implode at the next meal should immediately declare themselves "gluten-free"...

Well? Am I close? No? Then what the hell ARE you, gluten, if not an arse-muscle-attacking, human-killing machine from outer space?

Not going to talk, eh?

Fine, then. I WILL Google you. Please wait here. (Hum the tune "Girl from Ipanema" while you're waiting. I won't be long...)

Oh. According to livescience.com, it turns out you are the "proteins found in...endosperm" composed of "gliadin" and "glutenin," and you are potentially fatal to people with "celiac disease," which may develop with age due to "environmental factors"...

Jesus.

So I wasn't that far off, then.

    Yours truly,
    Steve Patterson
    Full of gluten

Dear personal exercise trainers,

I think exercise is good. I think having a person who knows how to exercise properly and can help motivate others is great. I'm just not sure how high a percentage of you that I have seen at "work" lately truly fall under these 2 categories.

Full disclosure: I have hired 2 personal trainers in my life. Both of whom I worked with only briefly. I certainly can't blame my lack of athleticism and fitness on them. I didn't give them much raw material to work with. Sort of like a mermaid trying to become a ballerina.

But I did notice a pattern in both of my trainers.

The first fellow (whose name I didn't even get in our one session together) couldn't understand that not everyone in the world was interested in entering into competitive bodybuilding. As such, each exercise he showed me was geared to "carving" my muscles. Now to some people, maybe even MANY people, I suppose carving muscles is the goal. Personally when I hear the term "carving," my mouth salivates like a Pavlovian dog, and I immediately picture and can actually *smell* a large portion of meat, ready to be carved, for my eating pleasure.

My other personal trainer, Tom, was (and still IS — I'm sure he's very much still alive) a fit, kind young man who better understood that I was just trying to achieve better general fitness, not worldwide bodybuilding domination. He showed me a number of "body weight" exercises that didn't require free weights since I explained to him that I spend a lot of time travelling and often hotel gyms are ill-equipped (literally, the equipment in them looks like it is suffering from illness). I even did my part in making the body weight exercises more challenging by having a generous amount of body weight to work with.

I would do the exercises Tom showed me while on the road, and then when I got home I would go back to the gym to have Tom show me more exercises so as to not "plateau." (An actual term in exercising, coined by the world's strongest Frenchman, Pierre Plateau. Untrue story.) But I couldn't stay motivated because working out "with" Tom was really just me working out while Tom yelled at me and counted in a way similar to how I do now with my infant daughter when she climbs stairs on her knees: "That's it, Scarlett...1!...Come on, now...2! One more......3! Good girl!" The tone was exactly the same when Tom worked out "with" me, only with slightly different verbiage: "OK, Mr. Patterson, and...1! Very good! Now bring it down, and push it back up and...2!" (Checks cell phone. I adjust weights incorrectly and drop a 45 pound dumbbell squarely on my sternum.) "...and 3! Good girl!"

Basically, being a professional personal trainer breaks down to being a professional personal *counter* who really couldn't be more uninterested in the results of clients.

I say this in general, and I'm sure there are great, highly interested personal trainers out there. Just not in my neighbourhood.

In my neighbourhood (the Junction, in West End Toronto) there are several gyms, with several personal trainers, who have taken lack of interest to a whole new level. Here, grown adults of varying degrees of fitness but a uniform degree of intelligence are constantly running up and down the street in what I've learned is called CrossFit exercises. They go back inside their respective gyms briefly, perhaps just to yell "O captain! My captain!" to their trainer. Then they reappear outside, running, which they could easily have done on their own, but this is all part of their "personal training," for which I'm sure they are paying a good sum of personal money.

I've even intercepted them on the sidewalk, offering to let them run around my house in circles for "half of what that other personal trainer is charging you." At which point some of them laugh, some of them (OK, the majority) look at me like I'm a sarcastic smartass (which I am), and a few have even seriously asked, "Well, are YOU a personal trainer?"

Don't worry, though. I never misrepresent myself.

I always answer, "Technically no. But I can count to 12 and yell at people while myself doing no exercise whatsoever."

My first client starts running around my house next week.

Yours truly,
Steve Patterson
Fellow "personal trainer"

Dear sports highlight shows,

I'm not sure what spell it is you hold over me, but you are the only thing on TV that I can watch, repeatedly, while falling asleep at night, only to watch again the second I wake up.

Why is this?

Ordinarily, once I've watched an episode of a show, any show, I don't need or want to see that show ever again. That rerun of *Seinfeld*...it was funny the first time. That movie with the Keyser Söze guy? HE'S Keyser Söze! Done and done. How-to shows? I only know "how-to" watch those once.

But you, you I can watch time and time again, fully knowing the outcome of each game, as well as every word that the sportscasters are going to say. Then I even re-watch the "expert analysis panel," made up of someone who played the sport professionally many, many years earlier, coupled with a non-athletic person who never did. Same formula for every show. Every night. And I watch it every time.

My wife thinks I am crazy for doing this. But, as I point out to her often, she watches a soap opera that seemingly will NEVER end even though you can NOT watch it for weeks or years at a time and tune in again without missing a single sentence of meaningful dialogue. She also watches reality shows like *Survivor*, which I can't stand for the simple reason that everyone at the end of that show is still alive. So the title is a bald-faced lie. My wife also regularly watches *Say Yes to the Dress*, a show about women choosing wedding dresses, even though she and I have been happily married for 4 years now. At least, I have been happy. (Note: Talk to Nancy about this.)

In any case, keep doing what you're doing, sports highlight shows, which is...wait for it...showing sports highlights. You keep showing them and I'll keep watching them. Religiously and repeatedly. Because either nothing else in the infinite kingdom of satellite channels can hold my interest, or you have combined with advertisers to hypnotize me and like-minded sports fans into mind-numbing complacency about your subliminal messages, making us consume things that we don't need and believe we are capable of things that we are not.

But that would be ridiculous.

Now if you'll excuse me, I need to order a new official game jersey of the Montreal Canadiens online, in case they call me up for a tryout this year. And I only have a few minutes before *SportsCentre* starts again.

Yours truly,
Steve Patterson
Professional athlete...watcher

Dear very, very drunk person thinking of getting "one more drink,"

I know you don't want to hear this right now (and you're incapable of READING it right now), but you don't need that drink.

How do I know this?

I've been there. On the precipice of total debauchery. Doing the drunk math that seems to lead to only one logical conclusion: "Well, if THAT many drinks made me feel THIS 'good,' then this next drink will make me feel even gooder!" (A very, very drunk word.)

It won't.

Here's what that next drink will lead to:

1. <u>Getting violent and obnoxious</u>: I know you're not "normally" a violent and obnoxious person, but the people you're about to get violent and obnoxious with don't. It's amazing how quickly this transformation can take place. You go from "pleasant and outgoing" to "violent and obnoxious" in a time span that seems instantaneous. It's not instantaneous. It's that "one more drink." Its ingredients might as well be "violence and obnoxiousness" (which I am convinced is why Seagram's has a whisky that is called VO).

2. <u>Getting violently ill</u>: Unless you are a masochist, no one would knowingly do this to himself (or herself — ladies can get very, very drunk too). Are you a masochist?... Sorry. I forgot you're very, very drunk right now. "Masochist" means someone who gets enjoyment out of what appears to be painful or tiresome. Let me put this another way: you don't want to puke on that rental tux, do you? Trust me, they'll charge you extra for the cleaning.

3. Embarrassing yourself in front of friends, family, associates or your boss: Once someone has seen you very, very drunk, it leaves an indelible image in that person's mind. An image that will be recalled whenever that person is thinking of you for a promotion, an important assignment or any future social gathering.

4. Sex with someone you shouldn't be having sex with: This is pretty self-explanatory, really, but very, very drunk people have very, very bad sex with other very, very drunk people that, once the following morning hits, is the WORST WAKE-UP CALL IN THE WORLD. And what makes it even worster (another very, very drunk word) is that the person you wake up beside has the exact same disgusted look on their face that you do.

5. Defecating (a.k.a. "pooping") in a non-traditional pooping location, such as a dishwasher, kitchen table or bathtub: It's not important how I know this. Just trust me, it can happen. And once it happens, it can't UN-happen.

So please, very, very drunk person, DON'T get that one more drink. Unless it's water. Get yourself a pint glass of water. Sit down until the room stops spinning. Then get yourself home, by yourself or with a less drunk friend (that there is no danger of having sex with).

You'll notice I didn't explicitly tell you not to drink and drive a vehicle. I'm assuming you know that. You're very, very drunk. You're not an absolute MORON, right?

Good talk. And good for you for taking the time to read this in the state you're in.

Your sober friend,
Steve Patterson

PS: If my friend James Lochrie is reading this, sorry again about your tub. It's been 23 years now, but I'm still very, very sorry.

This letter was written in the midst of the Canadian election in 2015. At a time when Stephen Harper was prime minister and Tom Mulcair appeared to have a very legitimate chance at becoming the new prime minister. Obviously that didn't happen. However none of this diminishes the accomplishments of Tommy Douglas, the abrasiveness of Stephen Harper or the stunning election victory of Justin Trudeau. I also still think Tom Mulcair is a man of strong character. He just wasn't strong enough for Canadians to elect him as their leader...

Dear Tommy Douglas,

I know you already know this based on your winning the title of "the Greatest Canadian of all time" in a CBC vote-in contest back in the year 2004, but honestly, what you did for this country is just, well, the greatest.

Accessible health care for ALL.

Next to hockey, the maple leaf and apologizing, it's the first thing people think of when they think of Canada (which I guess technically makes it the fourth thing people think of when they think of Canada).

Your radical and progressive idea of health care for everyone in Saskatchewan back in 1959 was viewed as dictatorial. (If you wanna see a true Canadian DICtator, may I present Stephen Harper?) And many doctors vowed not to accept your vision. Then a few short years later, it was such a success that it was adopted by all of Canada.

Bravo, good sir!

You spent your time in politics opposing stubborn, rich, short-sighted arseholes whose narcissistic tunnel vision couldn't be more deplorable if they were tentacled krakens rising up from the sea to consume a boatload of babies and puppies.

Fast-forward to the 2000s and you will be happy to know that there is a truly progressive leader in place in North America, who indeed shares your vision of "health care for all" and must fight daily battles against similar old, rich krakens.

Unfortunately, he is not the leader of Canada. He's the leader of the United States. Goes by the name Barack (even his name is progressive), and he is a black man...Yes, THAT happened.

What about Canada? Well, I don't blame you for not keeping up with what's going on here. For the last decade or so we've lost our way under the control of that aforementioned Harper fella, who, I'll be completely honest, I'm not even sure is human.

But on the bright side, the very party you founded, the NDP (yes, we still call it the "New" Democratic Party — sort of like "New" Hampshire, "New" Mexico or what old men call their "new" underwear), is currently led by a man named Tom Mulcair, who reminds me a bit of your story: strong leader of the opposition, lots of ideas and not afraid to fight. He even has a beard, which is as progressive as Canada is willing to get with their leading men...for now.

Can Tom take the party you started to the next level? Can Canada be represented by a truly progressive party that truly reflects the Canadian personality of "everyone deserves a shot at equality and those that have a little more should share with those who have less"?

I sure hope so, Tommy.

Because I don't believe that 21st-century Canada should be perceived as a country of closed-minded krakens, seemingly allergic to progress. The kind that you fought against your whole life.

They're hard to keep down, those old krakens. But kept down they must be. And yes, when they need it, we'll nurse them back to health as best we can. For free.

Yours truly,
Steve Patterson
Appreciative Canadian, who isn't afraid to get sick

Dear used household paint,

There's no denying your utility and beauty. You are the cosmetic make-up that makes otherwise dreary walls look fresh, vibrant and, well, "homey" (although some of you, if chosen incorrectly, can also make a home look homely — but I prefer to be a "paint can is half-full" kind of guy).

You are the one home renovation project that most homeowners can actually take on with a relatively reasonable chance of success. Sure a paint job gone wrong can be unsightly, but it's not as dangerous as a "knock-out-a-wall," "pretend-you're-a-plumber" or "let's-see-what-we-can-do-with-this-live-WIRE" job gone wrong is.

You are a good thing, household paint...

Until it comes time to get rid of unused portions of you.

Then you become a nuisance equivalent to peacefully disposing of nuclear-grade uranium.

What the hell is it about you that you can't be thrown in the garbage like everything else? I scooped up the remnants of a few gallons of paint left in the basement of my house when I moved in and left them on the sidewalk for garbage pickup. Well, neighbours couldn't have been more terrified if I had placed syringes full of tuberculosis/Ebola (tubercubola?) into bowls and labelled them "free juice."

I learned this after the garbage men gleefully left the cans behind while collecting other garbage that, in my opinion, was much more dangerous than leftover latex paint. It included: pieces of wood with nails sticking out, previously-enjoyed tissues that had a flu season's worth of snot in them and diapers full of sh—..."stuff" that you can't believe comes out of a beautiful little baby. All these dangers the garbage crew gladly took. But not you, used household paint.

Based on the reaction of the garbage men and my neighbours, I'm actually thinking of going into my local bank with a gallon of used paint just to see if the cashier will clear out the vault in sheer terror, shouting, "OH MY GOD! HE'S GOT USED PAINT! TAKE IT ALL, MISTER! JUST PLEASE, DON'T PAINT ME!"

I honestly don't know what it is that makes you so dangerous. Is it the same stuff that's in batteries? Namely, battery acid. Do you have battery acid in you, paint?

Most importantly, how can something that everyone purchases to <u>cover the inside of their house</u> become so immediately dangerous the second it is no longer in use? Are walls the antidote to your poison?

I don't expect you to answer because, for one, you can't talk. But more importantly, you're inherently dishonest in that your raison d'être is to cover things up.

Well, just know that I am on to you. I WILL get rid of you somehow, used paint. Provided I can Google "How do I get rid of used paint?" without triggering a crack squad from CSIS to be dispatched to my house and to command me to "slowly move away from the paint!"...

On second thought, that may actually be the only way to get rid of you.

Yours truly,
Steve Patterson
Unintentional paint hoarder

Dear Wolf Blitzer,

Of all the places to get situational news from, I like your *Situation Room* the most!

Partly because you guys seem to have complicated graphics at the ready for every conceivable situation, from "cat caught in tree" to "state governor caught in cathouse." But mostly because of you, Wolf.

First of all, your facial hair perfectly matches the hair on the top of your head. Not just the shade of it (it is one shade of grey — sexier than the other 49, if you ask me), but also the SHAPE of it. Thick and luscious around the cheeks and over the top of the head, separated only by your oversized spectacles, which seem to say, "Trust me. I read... a LOT." It's as if, before each situation breaks, your handler shaves off the thick grey hair that covers your eyes, you put your news goggles on, and it's WOLFTIME!

Which brings me to the question I have always wanted to ask you, and feel free not to answer this if it will compromise your position, but... are you an actual wolf?

I ask this not just because of the hair thing, but also because I know of no other human being named Wolf. Sure, there are a couple of Wolfgangs out there, like Wolfgang Puck. But somehow the "gang" part softens it. Like he's trying to be accepted into a group. Not you. You're a lone wolf, Wolf.

Furthermore, you are the only newsman I know of who is NEVER on the late-night news. Only afternoons and early evenings. Those are the only "situations" you cover. During the late-night news hours, you're on the prowl, aren't you? Sniffing out news. Howling at the moon. Getting to the true meat of the situation.

CNN couldn't risk you being on the 11 o'clock news because if the newscast went one minute over midnight, you might eat everyone else in the situation room. Which, let's be honest, would be a pretty incredible situation in itself. But then, who would report on it afterwards?

Anyway, I don't expect you to answer this question, and don't worry, I won't share my knowledge with others. Just know that I know what you are and I don't judge. As long as you keep bringing us those situations as they develop ... provided they develop in late afternoon or early evening.

Yours truly,
Steve Patterson
Wolf watcher

Dear Pope Francis,

I have to say, I like the way you pope.

Unlike your predecessor (who didn't even decease by the way, which is weird), Benedict the 16th (I called him "Benny the 1-6"...he never responded), you truly are the "people's pope."

At public events you forgo security that other popes before you wouldn't have been caught dead forgoing (pun intended). You wash other people's FEET, which is something I can't believe even aestheticians at spas do, let alone the leader of the Catholic church. You speak out on issues other popes never have, such as climate change, which is surprising because for once the head of the Catholic Church and the science community are on roughly the same page. And you have over 6 million followers on your Twitter account! I'm not saying you're bigger than Jesus, but as far as I know, He only had 12 followers (ba-dum-ching!).

Of course, not everyone agrees with the way you pope. Politicians say you should stay out of political affairs, scientists who have been paid off by those politicians say you should stay out of scientific affairs, and not surprisingly, when you highlight human rights atrocities in places like Syria, the people responsible for those atrocities tell you to mind your own business.

But that's what I like about you, Pope Francis: you see the whole world as your business, and I think you're absolutely right to do so. Those who don't want to follow the Catholic faith are free not to (unlike at times in history when they were NOT), and your opinions DO matter to millions of people based on their faith. Sure, those opinions may not always be exactly right (that whole "infallible knowledge" thing just doesn't work in the 21st century). But when you talk, people listen. When you apologize, it comes out as sincere. And if you stop talking, they might turn to an idiot like Dr. Phil. And that guy hasn't washed a single foot in his entire life, including his own.

So, keep poping the way you're poping, Frank! (I feel like we're friends now.) And give my regards to Benny the 1-6. God knows what he's doing (literally).

Yours truly,
Steve Patterson
The guy in the Canada T-shirt to your left in St. Peter's Square that one day

Dear Canadian men's soccer program,

I don't mean to kick you guys when you're down, but if I did, you should probably put me on your team, even though I've never played organized soccer.

At the time of this writing (July 20, 2015) you are ranked 103rd in the world, just below the country of Oman, as in "O man, I can't believe how low the Canadian men's soccer team is ranked!"

How is this possible?

The argument used to be that Canadians preferred hockey over soccer. And while that may be true as far as spectators go, I really don't think that is still true when it comes to youth participation.

Canadian boys do play soccer.

"But we don't play it year-round," you might say.

Let me read you the names of a few of the other countries listed above you in the rankings. Belarus is number 100. Finland is 90. Estonia is 82.

None of those countries are exactly considered to have "ideal soccer climates" either. And that last one highlights another mystery.

The population of Estonia is just over one million people and dropping. The population of Canada is 35 million and climbing steadily. And Estonia is 21 spots higher in the World Cup rankings?

In short, we are a large and growing country, with pretty lax immigration policies. And we can't gather together 11 GUYS WHO CAN KICK A BALL AROUND MORE EFFECTIVELY THAN A COUNTRY THE SIZE OF THE CITY OF CALGARY. I'll say it again: O man!

So what can be done about this?

Well, I'm not a soccer expert, but I would suggest that you encourage EVERY parent of EVERY young boy in Canada to sign them up for soccer right now. I'll wait here...

Next, let's bring in a coach who has had success elsewhere (even if it's just the guy from Belarus to start; I'm guessing he wouldn't mind spending the summer in Canada) to show our lads how it's done at a young age.

Finally, let's develop a more competitive environment in youth soccer, so we can find out who is actually good at it. This goes directly against the recent decision to NOT KEEP SCORE in youth soccer in Ontario. Apparently this has been done with "great success" in other soccer-playing countries. At least that's what we were told. But I think they were lying to us.

Not keeping score in sports is fine if you are: a) playing a game of "catch" with your children b) very bad at sports but still want to "exercise" or c) not tired of being embarrassed on an international stage in the world's most popular sport.

It's time for you guys to be embarrassed. It's time for you to set your sights on being better at soccer than some countries most of the world doesn't even know the name of. It's time to keep score, give away the personnel who haven't won and stop losing.

And let's set loftier goals than, "Maybe we can leapfrog Oman in the standings."

I'm not saying we should win the next World Cup. But it would be nice if, given our country's resources, we weren't at the bottom of the World Barrel.

That's all I've got for now. Please kick these ideas around and try not to miss the mark completely. Again.

Yours truly,
Steve Patterson

PS: I should point out that I am part of the problem, having always been a terrible soccer player. But this isn't about me. This is about Canada.

Dear Canadian oil companies,

I'm sorry President Obama said no to the pipeline that former Prime Minister Harper said was a "no-brainer."

I'm sorry that the current price of oil here in late 2015 is less than $40/barrel.

And I'm sorry that the current worldwide supply of oil is so vast that even if every Canadian buys matching SUVs and rides them like giant roller skates, we'll never be able to consume it all.

I understand that you are used to making millions of dollars every hour and that has now slowed down to about 8 bucks per day gross (literally and economically).

However, I write you not to point out the bad news, but to offer some good solutions.

It is time to think outside the barrel!

Sure, the Americans don't need or want our oil anymore, but you know what's worth more than our oil now? Almost everything, that's what! Including beer! Canadian beer is more per case than Canadian oil is per barrel. So I say, go ahead and build that pipeline. And if those "radical environmentalists" try to get in your way, tell them it's for good old Canadian beer! Then, if it ruptures and there is a spill... DELICIOUS! American men will line up to help with the cleanup, which will be completed faster than you can say, "Whoa! There's alcohol in this stuff!"

Or, you know what else we have a lot of? Maple syrup! Matter of fact, we source over 75% of the world's maple syrup. And guess who consumes 98% (approx.) of the world's pancakes? You guessed it: our southern neighbours. And who cares if that stuff spills on trees? That's where it came from in the first place.

Now, if you don't want to go through the hassle of building pipelines (and I don't blame you if you don't), you're going to have to convince

Canadians themselves to consume more oil domestically. Well, you know what Canadians love more than pipelines? Water parks! And you know what is more slippery than water? OIL!

You guys could start the first slide-filled "oil park" with millions of litres of non-stop, sweet, sweet crude flowing down slides and through "lazy rivers." (Hell, it wouldn't be the first time you guys got some in rivers, right?) And the best part is, oil is black and black is "slimming." So a man could be on the top of your oil slide looking like Mike Duffy and emerge looking like Denzel Washington!

What do you think? Not bad, eh?

I'm just trying to help.

Yours truly,
Steve Patterson
A pipeline of ideas

Dear "cloud" computing,

What are you?

I mean I understand the basic concept: you're "storage" for virtual computer data, right?

But if you are storing virtual computer data, then why in the world are you named after something in Earth's actual environment that is really just a collection of condensation? This association just doesn't...wait for it...hold water.

And you know what else you don't hold very well? Computer data.

I learned this after my "smartphone" (another questionable product name) sent me a message saying that my cloud storage was <u>almost full</u> and that I would have to purchase <u>additional cloud storage</u> for my apparently oversized amount of virtual data.

You see, this is why I never stored stuff in condensation before. Because it can't really HOLD anything.

Some say cloud computing is superior to storing data on a computer's "hard drive" because with the cloud you can access your information from "anywhere you are."

Well, here's the thing with that. I take my laptop computer with me pretty much wherever I go. So I already do what cloud computing does in an actual, physical hard drive. Hard things are better to store stuff in than clouds (slow me down if this doesn't compute).

Now I'm sure you'll try to argue with me based on the arguments I've had with the GPS system in my car over which route is the best one to take home. The GPS doesn't care about being stuck in traffic. To the GPS that's just more "quality time being helpful." In a similar way you, cloud computing, don't care how much money I have to pay for additional storage because you've never had to pay for anything in your life, and if anyone were dumb enough to try to store money in a cloud, it would be wasted immediately in the exact way that hip-hop stars figuratively brag about wasting it when they "make it rain."

So you tell your boss, presumably called something equally stupid, like Ms. Skyface, that I am NOT going to pay additional money for additional cloud storage because clouds are the worst things in the world to store stuff in! Even when the stuff you're storing isn't real stuff.

Yours truly,
Steve "Hard Drive for Life" Patterson

Dear knees,

In my childhood days, the worst that would happen to you would be I would "skin" you by falling down, which would quickly be cured by my mom kissing you, which, now that I think back, was pretty gross and damn selfless on my mom's part.

But now as I grow deeper into adulthood, I realize there are a myriad of injuries you 2 can suffer that not only can't be cured with a magical kiss from Mom but also, even though they can't be seen on the outside, can hurt like hell.

I learned this when I tore my "meniscus" in my left knee while running. Up until that point I didn't even know I had a meniscus. Let alone 2 of them. It sounds more like an event in the decathlon: "Up next, the men will throw each other through the air while spinning in the finals of the meniscus."

But I do have them, and I had torn one of mine. Which was revealed through an MRI that I lined up ASAP. However, since I am not a professional athlete, this took several months, during which time my torn meniscus got more torn. This despite the fact that I had only been running a few kilometres at a time at a slow pace, unlike in my old cross-country running days, when I would run much farther and faster without any injury whatsoever.

So I guess what I'm asking, knees, is why can't you guys hold it together for me here?

After getting my left knee surgically repaired, I went for about 2 years until I injured my RIGHT knee in exactly the same place (well, technically, a little to the right).

Now I'm awaiting another MRI to verify what I pretty much already know. It is scheduled for about a month from now at 2:00 in the morning! That's how busy the MRI place is. (Note to self: Open an MRI place.)

Apparently aging knees are like pieces of leftover roast beef: never quite the same as when they were fresh, and a little worse every day you ignore them.

Unlike the human heart, which is either perfect or suffers an "attack" and is then dead, the knees will deteriorate and deteriorate, daring you to try to run away from them, which of course you can't. Maybe I could just pray that you guys will get better. But of course that would require kneeling…which is quite uncomfortable for me now.

Man, I liked you 2 a lot better when you could be cured by a kiss from Mom.

Yours truly,
Steve Patterson
Torn meniscus survivor, hoping to keep running

Dear mermaids,

I'll admit it: I've been obsessed with you ever since I saw *The Little Mermaid* as a little boy back in 1989. (OK, I was 18 years old. But I was small for my age.)

The idea that there are beautiful women who live "under the sea" (great song, BTW) and spend their days frolicking around being adorable is almost, ALMOST enough for me to want to go fishing.

I also love that you wear either nothing or just a bikini top all the time. This makes perfect sense. You spend your entire lives swimming, so what else would you wear? A pantsuit? Please. Your job is to mesmerize sailors and deliver messages between the sea and the land. Not to try and become the first woman president of the United States.

What I didn't know about you ladies is that you first appeared in cave paintings during the Paleolithic period some 30,000 years ago (according to oceanservice.noaa.gov) and you also are referenced in Homer's *Odyssey*, which would be the one part of that book I regret not having read.

I also learned that in the ancient Far East, you were the wives of powerful sea dragons and served as trusted messengers between their spouses and the emperors on land. Really, girls? Sea dragon wife-messengers? In modern times, up above sea level here, that would be known as "trophy wives of old guys."

But to me you are classier than that. Sure, your siren song is beautiful and you are a testament to the positive health effects of swimming since I've never seen a fat mermaid, other than Ursula from *The Little Mermaid*. But she is an old, ornery sea witch, with a slow metabolism much like _____ (insert your own reference here).

One thing you mermaids don't do is open your legs, because you can't. That keeps you out of a lot of trouble and keeps shallow mermen away. Which is lucky for you.

Unfortunately, according to educational films such as *Splash*, when you venture out of water and onto dry land, you are capable of taking on human form with 2 legs and, I assume, a vagina. And that's when all the trouble starts.

So how do little mermaids and mermen get made, then? I don't know. I guess that explains why there aren't more of you.

I Googled this question and found that others had indeed Googled it before me. All presumably men. And I'm probably under government surveillance now.

So let me just say to you, thanks for being the sweet, innocent, mystical creatures you are. With intoxicating singing voices, salon-fresh hair and, if you don't mind me saying, a lovely set of seashells.

I hope those old sea dragons are treating you with the respect you deserve.

Yours truly,
Steve Patterson
Mermaid fan, from a respectable distance above sea level

Dear letter E,

I guess it's fitting that you have arguably the greatest exposure of all the letters of the alphabet, considering you start and finish the word "exposure."

But what is it about you that gives you so much more work than the other letters?

It's tough to get through even a single sentence without using you several times. Matter of fact, just writing the previous sentence, I used you 10 times, including 3 times in the word "sentence."

It could also be because you appear twice in the word "elephant" and everyone talks about "the elephant in the room," which symbolizes something people don't walk to talk about (which is rarely an actual elephant). So despite the fact that you are the most commonly used letter in the alphabet, you are also the one that most people "don't want to talk about," when you're not even there. Which is "pretty deep" (3 more of you right there).

More recently, you have become a video game rating, indicating that anyone who wants to can join in the fun, as in, "rated E for everyone." This association suits you. Not just for its inclusiveness but also because "everyone" is another triple-E word, like the aforementioned "sentence," and now that I've mentioned it, the word "aforementioned."

So keep up the good work, letter E. Once you think about it, thErE's no lEttEr that can bE usEd with grEatEr EasE.

SincErEly,
StEvE PattErson

Dear John A. Macdonald,

As Canadian prime ministers go, I think we can all agree, you were the first.

They say you never "forget your first," but since your 2 terms of office were in the mid-to-late 1800s, it's safe to say that a lot of people currently alive have forgotten and/or never knew what you did for this country.

So let's remind them, shall we?

You made modern-day "Canada."

That's a pretty big deal.

Up until you and your fellow "Fathers of Confederation" George Brown and George-Étienne Cartier got together, this country was considered a British colony, with a good degree of French influence, a group of Aboriginals who were here already and a vast area known as "Upper Canada," which wasn't even at the top of the place geographically. Essentially it was a weird Picasso painting that everyone knew was beautiful but no one quite knew why.

Then you came along and figured out that the only way to keep the country together was to have a way to GET together, which turned out to be the Canadian Pacific Railway, an incredible undertaking which required planning, skill, effort and sacrifice that in today's Canada would be unimaginable. Today we give people millions of dollars to build "websites" so that people can get on a "social network." (Don't ask, John. It's embarrassing.)

Then you walked into a conference in Washington (cleverly called the "Washington Conference") with Britain and the United States, where it was conceivable that Canada would be "gifted" to the United States. But instead you came out with Canada large and in charge and Britain willing to pay for this railway that would link the country together.

In today's vernacular, "You got game," good sir. Or, as your friend Cartier would have said, you've got "beaucoup de balls."

The rest, as they say, is still happening.

But the important thing is, if it weren't for you, John A. (your middle name, Alexander, is pretty cool by the way; I might have gone with that over John, but I'm nitpicking here), then this country that I know, love and LIVE in every day wouldn't exist. I would either be speaking in a British accent or screaming "U-S-A!" at every opportunity and hating myself for it.

So I just wanted to take this long overdue opportunity to say thank you, sir. Thanks for giving birth to a country that I hope never dies. And thanks for giving the nod to our Aboriginal people with the name Canada. If you were a real narcissist, I'd have to tell people that I lived in Macdonald's.

Yours truly,
Steve Patterson
Proud Canadian
Not popular in the States

Dear letter U,

I'm not sure what to make of you...U.

In today's impatient, illiterate system of short forms, U might be the most U-sed one-letter word in the world. As in: Are U coming over? To which I like to reply: "Maybe EYE am," just to up the letter count to the way it used to be.

It really is confusing, though, the difference between U and "you." Heck, I've been using "you" in letters to other letters, which, if read out loud, could just as easily be understood to be U.

So for the sake of clarity, for the rest of this letter, when I'm talking to U, I'll use "you." But I still mean U...you. (I'm so confused.)

Without you, universities wouldn't be able to identify themselves — such as U of A (the University of Alberta) or my alma mater, the University of Western Ontario, UWO. Or my favourite, the fictitious (so far) Tuktoyaktuk University in the Northwest Territories, which already has actual campus clothing advertising itself as "Tuk U"! (True story.)

Canadians have a special affinity for you, including you in many words that our American neighbours do not, such as "colour," "favourite" and, well, "neighbour." I'm not sure why Americans leave you out of so many words, but it makes you wonder whether it bothers them when people refer to them as "USA." Perhaps they would rather be referred to simply as "SA"? But then people would confuse them with South America, which isn't really "American" at all.

Back to you, U. You also seem to be relatively new to the alphabet in that examples of the old Latin alphabet seem to substitute the letter V for you in many words, such as "maximvm" or "maximvs." Why did the Latins do this? I don't know. But it's uery confvsing.

In conclusion, I like you, U. No matter what form you/U appear in.

Yours truly,
Steve Patterson
From me to U

Dear periodic table of elements,

You probably get this a lot, but you confuse the hell out of me.

From the symbol of "Au" for GOLD to "Fe" for IRON to my personal least favourite, "K" for <u>Potassium</u>, it's like you were put together for the express purpose of ensuring that people with a firm grasp on the alphabet never gain any understanding whatsoever of the elements. (Including what an "element" is. I thought Earth, Wind, Fire and Water pretty much covered it. And Water isn't even necessary if all you're doing is starting a sweet-sounding R & B band.)

Also, your general classification system for the specific elements is ridiculous. There are "poor metals" and "noble gases." What makes metals like Tin (Sn) and Lead (Pb) so poor, while gases like Helium (He) and Krypton (Kr) are "noble"? What is so noble about making human voices sound like chipmunks and KILLING SUPERMAN?

Then there are the "rare earth metals" which sound completely made up. Like "Es" for "Einsteinium." Really, guys? What does Einsteinium do? Come up with theories that make the other metals feel relatively stupid? Or "Cf" for "Californium." What does that do? Help you tan while waiting around for an inevitable earthquake to hit?

Honestly, I'm not sure who put you together or why they might have thought you would be a helpful guide. But if you ask me (and I know you didn't), all you've done is take things that were already confusing on their own and made them into one giant thing that is way more confusing.

Which, following your lead, I will summarize as an "ignoble gas" called Methane with the symbol: Pu.

Yours truly,
Steve Patterson
Emitter of "Pattersonium"

Dear PGA golfers,

Congratulations on getting so good at something that so many people do in so much of their spare time that it is your FULL-time job.

Well done, young (and old) men!

As a casual (read "terrible") golfer, I am torn between applauding your talent and persistence and making a working voodoo doll and stabbing it incessantly out of envy. For the record, I almost always choose the former.

From the classic legends like Arnold Palmer and Jack Nicklaus (whom I have confused so often with Jack Nicholson that I once credited him with a brilliant turn as "that guy in that *Cuckoo* movie") to the new young phenoms like Rory McIlroy and Jordan Spieth, I'm in awe that great golfers can be great when they are in their 20s and remain damn good well into their 60s.

In between the classics and the newest phenoms, of course, is Tiger Woods, the formerly young, formerly respectable man who set the golf world (and, as it turns out, quite a few cocktail waitresses' crotches) on fire in a torrid winning streak that seemed assured to break the record of 18 major championships set by Jack Nicklaus. (Note: Jack Nicholson hasn't even won 1.)

Then all hell broke loose when it was revealed that Tiger, despite being married to a beautiful Swedish woman and having 2 beautiful children and being the world's best professional golfer, decided to throw it all away because he couldn't keep his driver in his pants. Which prompted his now ex-wife Elin to take a few swings of her own with Tiger's clubs, which may, in fact, be the main reason he is no longer the best professional golfer in the world. Which would also be a great example of poetic justice.

But enough about him.

You guys are intriguing to me not just because of your skill, precision and consistency but because you sometimes screw up shots just like I do. Those are the moments I live for. When one of you tries to feather a chip onto the green and you end up driving it into the water, I'm sorry, but it makes my heart grow 2 sizes bigger with joy. Because it is in those moments that I can actually say, "Yep. Been THERE, my friend. Don't you hate it when that happens?" Followed by laughter because it's not me.

Yours is the only sport I can really do this in.

Baseball? Sure, sometimes they miss a routine pop fly or ground ball that I could have had or strike out horrendously. But this is balanced out by the fact that if I faced a pitcher that threw a 95 mph fastball, I not only would look silly swinging and missing but would probably urinate my pants. Hockey? I tried to take an effective slapshot once, fell down, pulled something and never tried again. Football? Let's be very clear here. The vast majority of football fans in the stands would be in the hospital if they played even one down with these gigantic creatures (kickers excepted). Soccer? I can't run very fast or kick very well. But I can writhe on the ground like I've been hurt with the best of them. And finally basketball...well, I would never be able to keep up with these extremely tall, extremely powerful people, but I can sink free throws with more efficiency than a surprising number of them. Which is why I feel OK yelling "You're a bum" at them from a safe distance away (i.e., watching them on television).

But golf? Golf I can do. I can get through a round without risk of injury or disfiguration. I know "which club" to use and it is often the same selection as the pros: "Hey, he's using his putter to putt! I do that."

In fact, in many ways, I work harder at golf than many of you pros do. Because while you are taking 60 or 70 shots per game, I'm taking well over 100. All of this while pleasantly drunk.

So please, keep it up, pro golfers! And keep it in your pants when it is down.

Because the hero status you somehow earn smacking a tiny dimpled ball around a course can, believe it or not, be overshadowed by being a horrible human being when you are off course.

Yours truly,
Steve Patterson
"Golfer"

Dear professional poker players,

Congratulations on forming a professional "sports" league from something that many people consider to be a <u>disease</u>. It gives hope for other diseases to form their own leagues such as the National Herpes League, the World Diabetes Association or Major League Lupus.

On the bright side, you have provided ample income for people whose opportunity to make a gainful living outside the poker world is severely limited.

I don't begrudge anyone becoming a success in their chosen activity, provided that it is not hurting anyone else and is legal. But IS that the case with professional poker leagues?

I certainly don't mean to paint you all in the same suit (though that would be a "flush," which I understand is pretty good in poker), but I've heard more than a few true stories of people (usually men with families) losing their life savings in games of poker. Maybe I'm overly risk-averse, but that seems a steep price to pay for a <u>game of cards</u>.

And that is what poker is: a game of cards. No matter how "skilled" you are at reading other players' "tells," strategizing your bets and studying the game, you're at the mercy of which cards you are dealt. Sure, it's an interesting microcosm of life (aren't we ALL at the mercy of what cards we are dealt?), but it's a microcosm that can be avoided by <u>not risking your family's future in a game of cards</u>.

What I begrudge most is that you are on my *SPORTS* channels. Poker is not a sport because poker players are NOT athletes. Period. Athletes are people who participate in an activity that requires movement beyond the bare minimum required to stay alive. Lugers and bobsledders get by on the technicality that they RUN at the top of the hill before sitting inside a sled and allowing gravity to carry them down. Curlers don't move much, but they are at least gliding on ice, pushing and sweeping.

(Yes, I realize this also describes being a school janitor in the winter. And yes, I also think that is more a "sport" than poker.)

Even darts, another game many people consider to be an affront to "sports" programming, is more physical than poker — because dart players have to flick their wrists, focus their eyesight and remain upright despite being hammered on horrible draft beer.

Poker doesn't require any of this. You are seated the whole time, barely moving for hours. Hell, for all I know you have naps between hands since half of you wear sunglasses while playing. (FYI, depending on the angle, your sunglasses may actually reflect what cards you have in your hand. I don't want to tell you how to do your job, but that seems stupid.)

So in conclusion, while it is "nice" that you've found a game that requires no athletic skills, relies heavily on luck and has been the downfall of many families, it might not be a bad idea to develop some other life skills. Like going "all in" on spending time with your family, for instance.

Yours truly,
Steve Patterson
I prefer cribbage

Dear racehorses,

I feel for you fine, majestic specimens. From the moment of your birth, when you start walking almost immediately (thus making us human babies look like helpless little turds by comparison), straight through your competitive racing days and up until we treat your sore leg injury with a gunshot to the head, you live a life of servitude.

Sure, horses it seems have always served humans. From Roman centurions to ancient Egyptian times to the "Wild West" to the current "Relatively Tame East," horses have carried humans and their heavy possessions on their backs. Literally.

And what do we do in return?

We put the smallest men we can find (along with the largest whips that they can find) on your backs, strictly for our entertainment pleasure, and then bet on which one of those little buggers can best whip you into a frenzy (even though you know damn well how to run your fastest in a circle without any "help").

It just doesn't seem right. You've given great service to us humans over the years and you deserve better than to be our entertainment to wager over now.

So here's what I would like to propose. Next time you are all lined up with those little men with the big whips on your backs, run out of the gate as you normally would for a few steps. Then, all of you stop suddenly and see who can throw their tiny man the farthest. Whoever does wins a prize, which is all the carrots you can eat and a nice relaxing foot rub.

We'll call it "jockey toss," and I think it could be a big hit. For everyone but the jockeys. But honestly, what have THEY done for humanity over the years?

Yours truly,
Steve Patterson
Friend of horses
Trademark holder of "jockey toss"

PS: Why do people say, "I have to piss like a racehorse"? I've seen you guys pee and I have never had to go THAT badly.

Dear senior citizens,

Maybe it's just me getting closer to your demographic and further from my youth, but I think it's about time the rest of us smartened up, gave you the respect that most of you deserve and started listening more to your stories.

After all, you've been through things like the "Great Depression" (one of the world's worst oxymorons), 2 world wars and immeasurable changes in government that all promised to be "better than the last." The worst thing most of my friends and I have been through is phones with cords attached to them and dial-up internet.

My own dad is now firmly within your ranks and, being of frugal background, has welcomed the world of seniors' discounts with open arms (even though he barely buys anything and can't really open his arms as wide as he used to). My mom, sadly, passed just as she was entering your ranks, but thanks to her gift of the gab was able to pass on many, many, many stories in her lifetime. It's sort of a lost art these days, long-form storytelling.

Nowadays those damn kids (I'm practicing for being one of you) would rather stare at a screen using short-form all day than sit down with an actual human being and hear stories. But senior citizens' stories are better than any video game for pure imaginativeness.

Sure, with video games, they can pilot rockets through space in 3D and blow up aliens. But what about sneaking up behind the car of the mean man next door and shoving a "cow patty" in his tailpipe? THAT is real fun and real danger. Or having to fend for yourself among 11 children at the dinner table for a piece of the food that had to be actually killed by your dad for dinner that evening? If today's kids faced those kinds of conditions, there would be a lot less "I don't wanna eat this" and a lot more "PLEASE, SIR, CAN I HAVE A PIECE OF THAT?"

There's also the pure entertainment of stories where children wearing no seatbelts get flung forward from the backseat into the dashboard when Dad is forced to stop suddenly "because the idiot in front of us was going too slow." Or the stories where Mom reveals not only that she drank during her pregnancy with you, but she drank AND "smoked like a chimney." And you turned out "just fine." This is trumped only by your grandparent revealing that the birth of your parent was a "mistake," but they just went with it because "that's what you did in those days."

Every family has a treasure trove of stories to share, from the oldest generation on down, that only you senior citizens can truly tell — extrapolating the truth where necessary, of course. (You didn't live this long to not use that imagination of yours.)

So to all those in their golden years out there, please persevere and keep telling those stories to younger folk. It will keep your minds fresh and ours open to the fact that there is life beyond fictitious "reality" on screens.

I say all this realizing not all of you are nice. Some of you have decades and decades of arsehole behaviour behind you that you have simply continued with in your old age. Well, I encourage you to tell your stories too. They're still entertaining. And you'll be dead soon anyway.

Yours truly,
Steve Patterson
Respecter of elders (that aren't arseholes)

Dear letter K,

I don't k-now about other people, but I don't like you.

Firstly, because as was just illustrated, sometimes you are silent and sometimes you are not. And sometimes you are silent and then not silent within the same word, such as in the word "knock-knock."

What the hell is wrong with you, K? You're either pronounced or you're not! Like a lisp.

Secondly, you have become a symbol of things you have no right to symbolize. Like a strikeout in baseball. There are several other letters to choose from in that word that would make a better short form than you. Like SO, for instance. But then, I suppose, "strikeout in baseball" would be an SOB, which is already taken. More importantly, though, when a pitcher gets 3 strikeouts in baseball and it is recorded for all excited fans in the stands to see, it looks like a group of racists have come out to the ballpark. Which is hopefully not the case.

And while we're on that topic, what a bummer of an organization that chose you to represent them: the Ku Klux Klan. I know it's not technically your fault, but you have to ask yourself, why did they choose YOU?

Similarly, why in the world are you the symbol for "potassium" on the periodic table of elements? You're not even IN the word potassium. It's like the name "Kardashian" (another bummer of a word that starts with you, by the way) being symbolized by a picture of a Rhodes scholar's brain.

I write all this not to be mean to you, letter K, but just to let you k-now that whenever you hide in cute words like "knit" or "knowledge," you are not fooling me. You are a devious racist, "striking out" against other more honest letters, and apparently you're riddled with potassium.

Yours truly,
Steve Patterson

Dear schoolyard bully,

I know this will be hard for you to understand, because you're currently overpowering classmates that you consider weak. But if you don't change course very soon, you're going to be the powerless, lonely, weak one.

How do I know this?

Because I've seen the people whose potential peaked in high school. They're easy to identify because they're still trying to wear their high school leather jackets at age 40 on their way to the unemployment office.

"Not me," you say. "I'll power my way to the top."

Here's the thing: there's more power potential inside your head than inside your biceps.

"Well, I'm going to become a professional athlete," you say.

Hey, if that's truly what you want, go for it. But becoming top-notch in sports and in life requires discipline, intelligence and — this is the important one — FRIENDS.

Do you have friends? Like, real friends. Not just minions that are afraid of you or fellow bullies who will turn on you faster than you can say "But wait! I thought we were friends!"

Friends are the people that get you through life. They stand not just behind you but in front of you. Especially in times when their friends are being bullied.

"Shut up, old man! You don't know what you're talking about. I'm going to punch you in the face."

Easy there, bully.

You're not. I'm speaking to you from the future. Your future. Which looks very lonely and bleak right now. Unless you have the strength to change it.

And that strength doesn't come from your fists. It comes from telling someone about what has turned you into a bully and asking for help. Asking for help is the strongest thing anyone can do. Closely followed by helping others out when they ask.

You probably bully others because you were bullied at some point. Maybe it was in your own home. You think it's your duty to pass it on. But it's not. You want to do something really strong? Ask for help. Stop the bullying. Become a friend.

Yours truly,
Steve Patterson
Punch lines are better than punches

Dear best friend Ted,

You've been my best friend for 35 years now. So I figured it was about time I wrote you a letter.

Ironically, given your occupation as a letter carrier, you may actually end up delivering this to yourself. So please don't lose this before it gets to you (which has been known to happen occasionally with Canada Post).

OK... so what does a grown man write to another grown man that he hasn't already said to him in 35 years of conversations?

As it turns out, I have a lot of unanswered questions, actually.

First of all, what is your favourite colour? I only remember you wearing school colours that were imposed on us in various uniforms over the years. I've never heard or seen you express a preference for any one particular colour, and I know for a fact I've never asked you. Apparently it's just not the kind of question a guy asks another guy over the course of over 3 decades.

Secondly — please be honest here — how many strokes do you think you've "creatively miscounted" off your golf scores in our years of playing against each other? For me I think it's about 25 in total. None of which have ever affected the outcome of a skins game of course. That would be an arsehole move. But just so you know, I'm not even as "good" as the bad scores I have recorded would indicate.

Third, how often do you think back to our childhood together and wonder how we made it to adulthood alive? Between bar fights, car accidents and other various near misses, I figure we've cheated death together at least a half dozen times. Thinking back to those times now makes me laugh the hardest. In particular the "brawl in Hull" that ended up being an inter-provincial battle where you described the incident to police using a crudely drawn diagram. That's one of my favourite Ted moments.

Fourth, you ever wonder if we would have stopped being friends at some point if things had gone differently? You could have become an NBA star. I could have become a professional baseball player. We both could have become exotic male dancers (if we both knew how to dance, were more attractive and exercised with any consistency). Instead, you stayed in London, Ontario, met and married an incredible woman who is one of the best people that I know in the world. Meanwhile I went off in search of fame and fortune in comedy around the world and landed in Toronto with mostly anonymity and a comfortable living.

Through all of that and all the people I've met, you remain my best friend. The one person I can trust with anything and know will never deceive me (except with golf scores).

I mean, of course, our wives are our "best friends" really at this point. But they weren't there during all that weird stuff growing up. Or there is NO WAY they would have married us.

Anyway, that's it, Teddy. Just wanted to say thanks for being the best friend a middle-aged man could possibly ask for. I'll write you another letter in another 35 years.

Yours truly,
Patterson

PS: By the way, my first name is "Steve."

Dear wife,

I suppose I should call you by your first name, but then the others who are reading this won't know who I'm talking about. There are lots of women named Nancy. There's only one I can call wife legally.

We've been married a little over 4 years now, and I can't speak for you, but for me it's been the best 4 years of my life.

Sure there are parts of those best years which aren't the best. Usually created because I am away from home too long making other people laugh and you are left behind with a crying baby.

I know this marriage may not be all that you signed up for when marrying a comedian. On paper it might have seemed like you'd spend every minute of every day convulsing in laughter. In reality you now know that the comedy business is not all it's "cracked up" to be (sorry). You especially know this because you are also my manager. So you field a lot of the calls that come in with weird comedy requests, even after almost 20 years as a pro. Requests like "Can Steve come do comedy while people are walking from a tent to inside the building?" or "Can Steve come do a show for one 100th of the rate he usually charges, or better yet for free, because it will be such good 'exposure' for him?" You respond to these requests with a great deal of professionalism and often even try to pass the gigs on to other comedians. Whereas if I were responding to these requests on my own, the tone would much more likely rhyme with "Go duck yourself."

Comedians have put up with all the pain that comes with comedy. Agonizing over the words that are supposed to be "instantly funny." Long hours of travel in unpredictable climates. (The Rocky Mountains are beautiful, but not when driving through them in the winter in a rental Toyota Tercel.) And having to perform for people who may or may not feel like a comedy show when you yourself don't particularly feel up to performing.

163

It's a challenge for me but a tougher challenge for you having to sched-ule things around my schedule. Like pencilling in time for us when the baby is asleep and both of us are both at home and not asleep. Or bearing the brunt of a performance gone bad (a grown man sulking can't be pretty). You also have to put up with my sarcasm at all times since, in your own words, "sarcasm bought this house."

So I just want to say, from the bottom of my heart and very honestly, thank you, dear wife. Or "Nancy" (if that's your real name). I know not every moment of our life together is ideal. But a lot of them are. Or at least they are to ME.

Now, let me know what you think of this letter once you've proofread it and sent it off to the editor, OK?

But first, the baby is…Oh. You've got her. Thanks again.

Love you,
Anonymous

Dear Malala Yousafzai,

There are a lot of impressive young people in the world, but none, in my opinion, as impressive as you are.

You stood fearless in the face of Taliban terrorists to fight for your right to an education in Pakistan. And what did your fearlessness get you? It got you shot in the head. Yet STILL you persevere in the face of oppression and terrorism. All of this while being a teenage girl.

To put this in some sort of perspective, we have young women (and young men) in North America who knowingly skip school just to "hang out." Yet if they were shot so much as an angry glance by someone who opposed them they would cower in fear. (I know this because I was one of those young men a long time ago.)

You have now inspired young women in oppressed countries, and by extension people around the world, to be fearless in their fight for equality.

For THIS you became the youngest ever Nobel Prize laureate in 2014 at the age of 17, and you were also granted an honorary doctorate from King's College in Halifax, Nova Scotia. Hard to say which one of those holds more international clout. And it is somewhat ironic because if there is one person in the world who would want to attend school and EARN their doctorate rather than be given it as an "honorarium," it is you. But hey, Canadians like to be nice and you have been through a lot, so please, just take it.

In any case, I am in awe of you, Malala. Of all the things to fight for in the world, education, knowledge and freedom are arguably the most important ones. If knowledge truly is power, you are well on your way to becoming one of the world's most powerful people. Which is amazing because a lot of the most powerful adults in the world right now don't seem very knowledgeable at all.

Here's to your continued fight for freedom and to being a truly inspiring figure for young women, young men and older men and women who may yet open up their minds and continue to educate themselves.

Oh, I almost forgot. I also heard you listen to Justin Bieber music. Of course that is your right. But I implore you, please, listen to other Canadian artists as well. There are others who may not be as commercially successful, but their music is quite a bit more, well, knowledgeable.

Yours truly,
Steve Patterson

Dear country songs,

I know the "hip" thing to do is to not like you. To mock you in fact.

As the old stories go, if your wife leaves you, your dog dies and you've got a pickup truck, then you've got yourself a country song.

But those stereotypes are outdated now. Just like the 8 track tapes that your songs used to be on (and that were, not surprisingly, a standard feature in many pickup trucks).

Today's country songs are more about love than loss. There is little to no mention of canine fatalities. And while pickup trucks still make frequent appearances, they are likely to be environmentally conscious "hybrids" that can comfortably seat a family of 5 with surround sound and video capabilities, rather than gas-guzzling chariots of loneliness for the angry man in the front and all his stuff in the back.

You guys (and girls — there are more women country stars than ever now) also often cross over into pop music, thanks to the pioneering work of stars such as Garth Brooks and Taylor Swift.

And let's not forget Keith Urban, who is now a judge on the mainstream music contest *American Idol* and who got married to Nicole Kidman, which simply would not have happened if his songs weren't at least palatable.

As I write this, there is a rumour that they are getting divorced very soon. But so what? He landed Nicole Kidman! A beautiful Hollywood actress, who is much taller than he is and whose former husband was Tom Cruise! If you are mentioned in the same sentence as Tom Cruise, well you are...Bad example. Point is, I don't think the country stars of decades past could have landed a Hollywood star as a wife for any amount of time. The exception being Lyle Lovett and Julia Roberts, which I still personally believe was an April Fool's joke.

Just look at the titles of today's country hits:

"Angels and Alcohol" by Alan Jackson

(I've always wondered what would happen if those 2 things were combined. It's the heaven of being hammered.)

"Anything Goes" by Florida Georgia Line

(That's very open-minded. Especially for people from Florida and Georgia.)

"Ignite the Night" by Chase Rice

(If you've got pyrotechnics and a dark sky, you've got a great party. Period.)

Now contrast that with some of the classic country stars' songs:

"He Stopped Loving Her Today" by George Jones

(Really, George? This is an occasion worthy of a song? How long had you been planning to stop loving her for?)

"The Gambler" by Kenny Rogers

(I've always said that gambling is a dangerous addiction. In this song it's mixed with alcoholism and — spoiler alert — the guy DIES at the end. Very depressing.)

"Crazy" by Patsy Cline

(We don't use that word anymore, Patsy. Now we refer to those types of people as "eccentric" or "differently normal." And it's not "crazy" to love someone. Unless it's a freak that's been planning on not loving you back for some time. Let's call him George.)

In conclusion, country songs, while I do admit that I used to be one of the people that made fun OF you, I now admit to being someone who has fun WITH you. I credit this change to your evolution from despair into joy, the attractiveness of your singers (Tim McGraw is a handsome man) and the life lessons that could only come from country music, as in Mary Chapin Carpenter's 1992 classic: "Sometimes you're the windshield, sometimes you're the bug." It's so TRUE, Mary. So true.

Yours truly,
Steve Patterson

PS: I've actually written my own country song called "Lonesum Star" about life in Canadian comedy. If you guys want to hear it, let me know.

Dear fishing,

I understand you've been around a long time and you'll probably be around a lot longer, but I thought you might like to know why I don't like you.

I don't like you because you're not a fair fight.

You put humans with massive rods (grow up), hooks and sometimes even harpoons up against completely defenceless fish. Then, you throw in the "middle man" of live bait, usually worms, which are pulled apart by otherwise mild-mannered people before their half-bodies are impaled on a hook, just to attract the unsuspecting fish.

In essence, you force people who otherwise might never kill a living thing to rip apart one living thing and then impale its half-part (talk about insult to injury) all in the pursuit of killing another living thing.

But what about "catch-and-release" sport fishing, you say?

As far as I'm concerned, that's worse.

This is where you do all the same preparations with massive hooks and live baits with the goal not of catching, killing and eating the fish but simply catching, maiming and then releasing the gravely injured fish back into the open water — where it will almost certainly be eaten by other creatures that it could have gotten away from had the arsehole human not maimed it for his or her own "sport." That's roughly akin to, instead of butchering a cow for a family to eat, going out into a cow field and throwing darts at them, then watching the poor things stagger around for a while. Which I guess is pretty much "bullfighting." Which I also don't agree with.

But hey, you have a LOT of fans. People who buy expensive equipment and massive boats and enter contests, desperate to catch a fish they can proudly pose for a photo with: "Look at this fish that I 'caught.' He was just out swimming around and I lured him in with some food on a hook, then yanked him out of his natural environment, which he of course can't live in. Best day of my life!"

Yes. And the WORST day in the fish's life.

Obviously you don't see it this way. You see yourself as a way of further enforcing the food chain. Humans are higher up on it, therefore we deserve to be the fishers and not the fishees.

But given the horrible odds (worse even than some casinos) do you see how what you're doing might provoke a massive retribution from fish, should the food chain ever be flipped?

Fish were around before humans, after all. They adapt better than we do. The day of aqua-reckoning may not be far away. And I have to say, I'm pulling for the fish.

I envision a time in the not-too-distant future, where in an underwater lodge a large bass fish (let's call him "Mr. Bass") proudly points to a framed photo of himself holding a dead fat guy up by the collar of his Ed Hardy shirt and says: "Oh I remember this one. I put a hook into a cheeseburger and then put it on the sidewalk in front of a sports bar. This guy picked it up and tried to eat it in one bite. He wasn't easy to pull in. Very heavy. And sweaty. But eventually I pulled him down and hit him on the head with a hammer. Which didn't knock him out at first. He just asked if I had any ketchup. So I shot him. Best day of my life."

THAT is why I don't like you and don't participate in you, fishing. And also why I never pick up seemingly free, delicious cheeseburgers off the sidewalk.

Yours truly,
Steve Patterson
Friend of the fish

Dear hockey,

Just to be clear here I mean ICE hockey. Which goes without saying in Canada, the United States and other ice-hockey-playing nations but has to be specified in non-ice-hockey-playing nations where they think "hockey" means field hockey. Which is obviously ridiculous. How can you even play hockey on a field? There's no ice.

Anyway, with my being a Canadian, it probably won't surprise you to learn that you are my favourite sport to watch. To be honest, I'm not even sure how anyone can make any comparison between you and the other major sports.

Sure, soccer players are in excellent cardio-vascular condition and run several kilometres per game. Basketball players have to endure knee-wrecking punishment on the "hard court" for years and are forced to try their jump shots over the reach of freakishly gigantic people. Football is a very tough game played by very tough men. (Except for the kickers. And the guys that hold their balls. [Rim shot.]) And baseball is great at playoff time, but for the 162 games preceding that, well, it tends to drag a little.

Here's the thing: even the most elite athletes in those other sports probably could not even STAND UP on skates, let alone do any of the other things on ice that professional hockey players do. They would look like fish out of water or, more accurately, rank amateur non-athletes on frozen water.

This simply can't be said the other way around.

A lot of professional hockey players warm up for their games by playing soccer. A lot of them could hold their own in a game of basketball (not for long, mind you, because they would foul out for body-checking in the first 5 minutes). As for football, they could throw, catch and run with the ball better than most, I'm sure (as long as those linemen didn't get a hold of them). Same for baseball. And as for golf, well, that's what a lot of hockey players do as soon as their hockey season is done, and some of them do it very well.

Add to this the fact that pretty much every hockey player on a team plays at least a few minutes in every game, while there are many players in those other sports who see as much playing time as the fans in the stands.

This makes hockey the most all-around team sport in addition to being the most all-around skilled sport in addition to being the most overall in-motion sport, which I would argue is what makes sports different from idly standing around.

So, just in case you need someone to speak on your behalf should a "which sport is the best sport to watch" debate break out, just know that you can call on me. I'm pretty good at debating.

Yours truly,
Steve Patterson
Great hockey watcher, horrible hockey player

Dear last piece of food on the tray at a party,

I'm not sure what happened.

You came out on a tray full of equally delicious pieces that looked exactly the same as you. Yet those pieces were devoured immediately by gluttonous guests and you remained behind, alone.

Why?

Is there something wrong with you that everyone else knows but I don't? Did your "best before" date just pass by in the last 3 minutes? Did someone take one bite of you and then put you back?

Maybe this only happens at parties in Canada, where every single person is exceedingly polite, so no one wants to be the one to take the last piece?

Is it rude of me to even be thinking of enjoying you? Would the other guests look at me like I was an arsehole the second I popped you into my mouth? Or, would it be MORE rude to not take you, thus leaving you out here in the open to tempt other guests into this same inner turmoil that I am currently experiencing?

I just don't understand how every other morsel of the giant tray of food you came from was consumed so ravenously and then, the moment it was just you, all the momentum stopped. A couple of people who were clearly about to reach for you acted as if they weren't even thinking about it.

"Please, Jim, you have it."

"Me? No. I am STUFFED. You should take it, Wendy."

"No, I couldn't. I want you to have it."

Then they both laughed and walked away, neither of them taking you.

Bringing us to our current standoff. You there, all alone, perhaps afraid and paranoid, wondering, "What is wrong with me? Why did they take all the others and no one wants me?" While I sit staring at you wondering what you are thinking.

Well, this is ridiculous. I don't want others to go through this. Get ready to get in my belly, you delicious-looking little —

And that's when Brett came up and casually shoved you into his mouth without so much as an "Oh, Steve, did you want that?"

Brett, as you now know, is a total arsehole.

Yours truly,
Steve Patterson
The guy at the party staring at the food

Dear "meteorologists,"

I know you've got a weather forecast to get wrong, so I won't take up too much of your time. I just have one question: where are the meteors?

A climatologist studies the climate. It's right there in the name. A geologist practices what he or she learns in geology. A proctologist looks into people's ... OK, bad example. But two out of three isn't bad.

But you get my point. If your job is to report on the weather, why are you called <u>meteor</u>ologists?

Why not weatherologist? Or whether-or-not-to-wear-a-jacket-ologist? I would even settle for wind-ologist since it feels like most weather is brought on by wind.

But the presence of "meteor" in your job title brings to attention the glaring absence of meteors in your forecasts.

It really bothers me.

So much so, in fact, that if I were to tune in to a weather forecast and hear, "THERE IS A METEOR RACING TOWARDS EARTH AT ONE BILLION MILES PER HOUR AND WE ARE ALL GOING TO DIE," my honest reaction would be, "Finally! The meteorologist talked about a meteor!"

But of course, if an apocalyptic meteor were actually hurtling towards Earth it would most likely be the main story and would therefore be read by the main anchor, who is known more formally as a "journalist." Yet they NEVER read from their journals. Which is a whole other pet peeve of mine.

Turns out the only ones on the whole news team whose job title makes sense are the sports reporters. And yet they are the ones the others think are "wacky."

Weird.

Yours truly,
Steve Patterson
Comedyologist

Dear procrastinators,

I know the fact that this letter is completed says otherwise, but I'm one of you.

Don't worry, I first thought of writing this several years ago, but I never got around to it.

What happened, you ask?

LOTS! First of all, on the day I sat down to write this, the sun came out. It hadn't been out in quite a while, you see (the sun is a bit of a procrastinator too, sometimes), so I had to get out and enjoy it. Then, when I came back inside, I realized that the plants I had been meaning to water for some time were dead. So I watered them.

Then 2 years passed, during which I was late for approximately 342 meetings, completely missed about 17 different family birthdays and was almost late for a comedy show (you have to draw the line somewhere).

I took out my laptop on a train ride, ready to write to you again. But then I stared out the window of the train, which was very relaxing, and I fell asleep for the rest of the 5-hour trip.

Three more years passed.

I went through 2 romantic relationships, said goodbye to a car I had forgotten to put oil in and called a friend in Australia I had been meaning to call for 6 years. Seriously. He said to come for a visit. So I did.

On the 14-and-a-half-hour plane ride to Australia, I thought of writing to you again. But I was too excited to be going to Australia. Then I watched 5 movies.

Six more years passed.

I moved to Montreal, fell in love, got married, wife had a baby, got approached by a publishing company to write a book of letters from my standup act. Wrote 82 other letters before remembering to write to you.

So what is the point of this letter? Well, I guess it's this: thank God that God isn't a procrastinator. Otherwise the creation of the world wouldn't happen for another 3000 years. And then this letter would have taken even longer to write.

Yours truly,
Steve Patterson

PS: Remember to write a PS for this before sending it.

Dear Sir Paul McCartney,

If there is one musician in the world who does indeed deserve to be called "Sir," it is you.

Not just because you are British and that is what your people seem to do whenever one of you reaches a certain age and has accomplished a certain number of things, but because — dammit, Sir — you just keep going!

From your place in the greatest rock 'n' roll band of all time to forming a successful band with your wife (which I didn't even think was possible, given the experience of one of your former bandmates), to your ongoing solo career, you are simply the greatest incarnation of a rock/pop musician that has ever lived.

Sure your voice doesn't have quite the range that it once did, you've had marital heartbreak, and you insist on maintaining the "mop-top" look for a hairstyle, including inexplicably being the only senior citizen with chestnut brown hair (for all I know your hair is an actual mop). But none of this matters once you start singing "Hey Jude" or "Get Back" or the now ironic "When I'm Sixty-Four."

Your music brings people back to another time. Or for some of us, takes us to a time we weren't even around for the first time. You are truly timeless, sir. Which is why it won't surprise me if you don't take the time to read this letter.

But in case you are reading it, on top of everything else, let me just say that if it ever came down to a Knight fight between you and "Sir Elton John," I would bet everything I have on you. He has about as much hope against you as a . . . wait for it . . . candle in the wind.

I'll let myself out. Good talk, Sir.

Yours truly,
Steve Patterson

PS: Do you have a mailing address for Ringo?

April 1, 2015

Hey, neighbour!

The other day you left your door open, so I went ahead and let my-self in. Saw your wife changing. She's a beautiful woman......APRIL FOOL'S! (She's not that beautiful.)

Gotcha!

Seriously, though, she is quite lovely. I'm Catholic, so I'm not allowed to "covet" her. But if I was...Woohoo! She could consider herself totally coveted.

Anywho...I'm writing to invite you and your family, whatever your names are, over to our place for a little meal or some drinks — you know, just to spread some cheer and get to know you folks. We're both responsible tax-paying parents. We practically share the same wall. So wouldn't it be nice to get to know each other better?

I sure think so.

Well, I guess that's it. Just drop a letter in our mailbox when you get this (since I'm not ready to give you my phone number or email just yet) and we'll try to work something out.

Hope to hear from you soon!

    Your neighbour,
    Steve Patterson

PS: Oh, almost forgot. It's APRIL now. Time to take down your fucking Christmas lights. Seriously.

Dear doctors,

There's no denying that many of you do good work. Great work. Miraculous work, even. Yet the expression everyone knows is "LAUGHTER IS THE BEST MEDICINE," so...nice try.

That's why I became a comedian and not a doctor. I wanted to provide the world with the best medicine possible: smartass observations.

Also, being a doctor seems to require a lot of work.

Especially if you're a medical doctor and not just a person who gets their "doctorate" in something and then tries to call him- or herself a doctor. Like "Dr. Phil."

Still, I empathize with you for the fact that even when you are not technically "on call," you are expected to do your job at a moment's notice. Such as when there is a medical emergency in a restaurant and someone yells, "Is there a doctor here?" You are professionally obliged to say, "Yes, I'm a doctor," and to try to help the person in need. This is exactly like when someone finds out I'm a comedian and immediately demands I "say something funny."

The difference, of course, is that while you are professionally obliged to offer medical assistance because of the Hippocratic Oath, there is no such professional obligation from a comedian. Which is why I don't eat dinner with private groups that I am performing an after-dinner comedy show for. They want me to make them laugh while I am sitting there eating with them. And you and I both know that is a dangerous choking hazard, which would require your attention. So...you're welcome.

Speaking about the Hippocratic Oath, I was taking a look at it (just in case I decide to become one of you after all) and it is interesting, to say the least, including this promise:

> To hold him who has taught me this art as equal to
> my parents and to live my life in partnership with
> him, and if he is in need of money to give him a share
> of mine, and to regard his offspring as equal to my
> brothers in male lineage and to teach them this art — if
> they desire to learn it — without fee and covenant...

Maybe I'm missing something, but I don't see a lot about medicine in there. This seems to just be Hippocrates' retirement plan and a free ticket to medical school for his MALE kids. Which seems to go against the idea of helping out ALL people who are sick and treating people equally when you're only obliged to pass on your doctor knowledge to men. Was Hippocrates a hypocrite? (Makes sense, I guess.)

Fortunately, the Hippocratic Oath was updated in 1964 to read as follows:

> I will respect the hard-won scientific gains of those
> physicians in whose steps I walk, and gladly share such
> knowledge as is mine with those who are to follow.

That seems much more inclusive. Common sense. So who, you may wonder, is the person that evolved the oath of Hippocrates? The dean of the school of medicine at Tufts University, a man named...wait for it...Louis Lasagna. Not even "Dr. Louis Lasagna" because no one would ever go to that doctor, because he sounds like an Italian porn star.

I guess what I'm saying is, maybe it's best you men (and WOMEN) don't take the words of Hippocrates or "Louis Lasagna" too literally.

Because while it would be nice to learn some know-how from you, I think I speak on behalf of all non-doctors in saying that if there's something wrong with me medically, please just fix it. You don't need to show me how you did it.

It's the same in comedy. No one wants you to explain a joke. They just want to laugh.

After all, that is the best medicine.

Yours truly,
Steve Patterson
Best Medicine Practitioner

Dear lawyers,

Look, I know your profession gets a bad rap. Mostly through bad jokes such as:

> "What do you call 1000 dead lawyers at the bottom of the sea?"

> "A good start."

Well that's just hurtful. I'm sure that of those 1000 hypothetically dead lawyers in this "joke," there were at least 10 really nice people.

Full disclosure (I wanted to speak your language in this letter): I have a lot of good friends that are lawyers. Mostly because one of my closest high school buddies went to law school at McGill University, so I attended a lot of parties there.

Since then, I have gone on several road trips with him and a bunch of lawyer friends, and they have always been very enjoyable. Sure, that's largely due to the large amount of disposable income they have. But I also find every one of them to be fun-loving, non-judgmental (they're lawyers after all, not judges) and intelligent company. Also, we tend to "bend the law" sometimes, so it's nice to have a network of people right there who can bail you out, either with sound legal advice or actual bail money.

But I guess most complaints about lawyers stem from their on-the-job behaviour, not their on-vacation behaviour.

And that I can totally see, based on my experience with one of you who is, far and away, the most corrupt "professional" I have ever come in personal contact with.

I won't name him here directly, because he would sue me, so let's just call him "Dick Fartface."

Fartface specializes in entertainment law, a particularly predatory field since many entertainers have contracts put in front of them for spec projects that may never come to fruition (and therefore may never yield any actual income). Yet these contracts are always geared towards divvying up income that doesn't exist and usually leaving the performer (on whose idea the entire project is based) with little to nothing.

So entertainers need entertainment lawyers to "fight on their behalf."

In this particular case, I called Dick Fartface not even for a contract that affected me directly but on behalf of a friend because I had heard he was a hard-nosed lawyer who was "good to have on your side."

As it turned out, he was hard-nosed, all right. He wanted to not only represent my friend as her lawyer but also to become her full-time manager and be entitled to a percentage of all of her income.

Before I could recommend otherwise, this friend had signed a contract with Dick Fartface that was worse than the contract already in front of her and had to pay a severe penalty to get out of it. Rather, I paid the penalty, because I had brought Fartface in contact with her.

Interesting lesson learned.

Should I have done more "due diligence"? Absolutely.

Should my friend not have signed a contract so quickly? No, your honour, she should not have.

But is it too much to ask that someone in the small world of Canadian entertainment law not be a complete and total Dick Fartface, whose reputation will certainly lead to a karmic correction in the not-at-all-distant future?

No, I don't think that's too much to ask at all. So watch your back, Fartface. Karma is coming for you...

But again, that's not ALL lawyers. That's just one guy — and, statistically speaking, given how many lawyers there are in the world, perhaps about one million other lawyers.

The rest of you are good people whom I would gladly vacation with any time.

Yours truly,
Steve Patterson
Friend to many lawyers. Enemy to one.

Dear baby Scarlett,

As I write this, you are in your room down the hall and your mom is trying to get you to go to sleep. But you are resisting.

I'm not sure why you don't like to go to sleep, but apparently it's pretty common among human babies. Your mom always blames it on me being a "night person." So naturally it's the part of your DNA that is mine encouraging you to stay up late. (Note: Your mom is not a scientist.)

You are 9 months and 2 days old right now. I look forward to the day when I don't have to count your age in months, since it will make you feel very old once you hit your 40s and in terms of months you will be well into your 400s. But I also dread the days when you won't just be sleeping down the hall and needing Mommy and Daddy to make you feel safe.

I understand that shortly after you start talking, odds are you will start "talking back," and I will long for these days when all that comes out of you are adorable little sounds. (From one end, at least. Far less adorable stuff comes out the other end.)

Anyway, I guess I'm just writing to say thank you for coming along and making your mom and me very happy. It might not seem like it at times. Like when I say no to you attempting kamikaze jumps off the bed, or "ouch" when you punch Daddy in the throat or a word I don't want you ever to repeat when you stomp both of your tiny (but deceivingly HEAVY) feet on Daddy's "special spot" first thing in the morning. But one flash of your smile and I forget any pain and, for that matter, most troubles in the world. This is going to be challenging when you get older and ask me for things. Unless you continue to kick me in the groin. In which case, you're not getting anything.

Your mom, she loves you more than I've ever seen a person love another person. Most mommies do love their little ones an awful lot. But I'm telling you, kid, you won the mommy lottery.

As for the daddy lottery, well, I think you're doing not too badly. There are daddies who are better at building things and fixing things and daddies who have more money and more hair. But I promise you right now, little one, there is no daddy who will try harder to be a really good dad than I will.

I'm sorry I have to be away a lot for work. Maybe by the time you can read this, I'll have built a comedy club at our house and I can be a "stay-at-home comedian." I'm also sorry in advance for any "dad jokes" that will embarrass you in front of your friends. But that is just part of the dad job description.

I love you more than almost any other girl in the world, Scarlett (you're tied with your mommy). I hope to keep you smiling and laughing every moment that I can for as long as I can.

I can't wait to watch you grow and share the joy you bring to me with everyone you come in contact with.

Now…can you please go to sleep?

Love,
Dad

Dear sliced bread,

You're a good thing. At times even a very good thing. But the benchmark against which all the "greatest" things should be measured? Come on. We both know this just isn't true anymore. Matter of fact, I would argue that it never was.

Don't get me wrong. I like bread as much as the next person. And yes, if I happen to get a loaf from a place where it is not already sliced, then I request that it be sliced. Because sliced bread is better than tearing it from the loaf with your teeth like a vulture eating roadkill.

So I would agree with the phrase "Sliced bread is slightly more convenient than non-sliced bread."

But "greatest thing" since you? At what point in history was that true?

Of all the great things to be created...The wheel, the car, the airplane, the space shuttle (and that's just modes of transportation off the top of my head). There's also plumbing, electricity and of course, clap-on, clap-off electricity (a.k.a. "the clapper"). The crapper and the clapper are both far greater than you.

Then there's the field of medicine. Insulin, aspirin, penicillin. Maybe these things aren't as handy as you if all a person is trying to do is sop up some gravy on a plate, but in the grand scheme of things, they all deserve strong consideration over you.

I tried looking up "the greatest thing since sliced bread" on the internet (also greater than you), and I found out that bread has been around since the "Neolithic period" (whatever that means), that Wonder Bread has also been around almost that long and that the first effective bread-slicing machine was invented by Iowa-born Otto Frederick Rohwedder and put into service in 1928 by the Chillicothe (Missouri) Baking Company. Which was so revolutionary that it made the front page of the local paper.

Wow. So you made the front page in Chillicothe, Missouri, eh? Well, no further questions then.

Giving you the benefit of the doubt, I looked up other inventions in 1928, figuring the competition must have been pretty weak that year. I found out they included the ice-cube tray (better than you at most parties), the electric razor (I still prefer a reliable blade) and...penicillin!

Are you kidding me?

So somehow you got people to believe that you were greater than life-saving medicine? This is ridiculous. Who do you think you are, sliced bread? Kanye West?

Yours truly,
Steve Patterson
Funnier than most loaves of bread

Dear people writing on their laptops at Starbucks,

I don't mean to bother you, since I see you're working on something very important, but if you don't mind, I have some questions.

First of all, are you working on a screenplay? I keep hearing of people who write screenplays in Starbucks, but I never hear anyone thank Starbucks in their Academy Award acceptance speech. Which is weird because you are using a lot of their electricity, and without their coffee it's unlikely you would even be awake right now. I also wonder what it is about the Starbucks environment that screams "movie inspiration"? Unless the movie is about a person who spends their entire day writing on a laptop at Starbucks. But who would go see that?

Or perhaps you're writing a book? This is a little more believable since a lot of people sit down to read books at Starbucks while drinking a coffee. So what better way to get inside prospective readers' heads than to sit and write it in the very spot where they might sit and read it? And you're drinking coffee too! Or, at least it looks like you <u>did</u> drink a coffee and finished it some time ago, and now you're just writing, completely oblivious to the people who just bought coffee and are now looking for a place to sit down and drink it.

If not a screenplay or a book, maybe you're creating an "app"? I've never understood how those are created myself or how they make money, since I've never paid for one. I figure the ones that are free are good enough for me. Do you have that one, Shazam, that figures out what song is playing just by you holding up your phone to listen to it...then it tells you the song, who sings it, where you can download it and where the musician is playing next? That thing is wizard-like awesome! And it's free. If you can create an app like that and offer it for free, I will buy you a Starbucks coffee (which is pretty good money for some of those apps). If you want an idea, how about "app-a-chino," which would turn your smartphone INTO a coffee! Genius, right? Good luck with it.

Well, I guess that's all the questions I have for now. I'll let you get back to whatever you're working on, and I'd better get back to this "book of letters" I'm writing. I'm just finishing up a letter where I wonder what the other people who are writing in this Starbucks are writing. When you think about it, that is the most logical thing you could be writing in a Starbucks.

Yours truly,
Steve Patterson
The guy writing with you guys

Dear letter X,

You are clearly the most mysterious letter of the alphabet.

First, out of all the letters that could have been chosen to exemplify mysterious, unexplained events, you were chosen for *The X-Files*. That's a lot of responsibility for a lot of weird stuff.

Secondly, you are the symbol of democracy during election times, with the placing of one of you beside a candidate's name meaning he or she is our choice. Even people who don't know how to write their own names or any other letters know how to make you. Pretty powerful stuff.

And when it comes to medicine, they could have combined that freaky "see-through-your-skin-ray" with ANY letter, but they chose you. Why? Because no one truly understands how that thing works, but we know to cover our genitals when going thru X-ray machines, lest they be mistakenly sent to another dimension.

But the greatest proof that you are the most mysterious letter is your existence inside all human beings in something called "the X chromosome." X chromosomes span about 155 million DNA building blocks and represent approximately 5% of the total DNA in cells.

More importantly, though, when 2 X chromosomes are present, FEMALES are created, while X and Y chromosomes combine to create males.

And females are far more <u>mysterious</u> than males.

Not unlike *The X-Files*, the 2 females/double-X-chromosomes that I live with (one of whom I actually had a small part in CREATING) mystify me every day with their ability to change tastes, likes and dislikes, and furniture/toy arrangements around the house. My daughter in particular can go from "loving" a food to hating it so much she must THROW IT AT THE WALL in a span of nanoseconds. The little boy babies I have seen don't do this. They eat everything constantly. Just like me. Apparently the Y chromosome controls appetite.

Meanwhile my wife, an adult double-X-chromosome, has articles of clothing that alternate between "It's perfect" and "It's hideous" based solely on how quickly I react or do not react when she puts them on. Us Y-chromosomers don't do that. Once we stop growing, we are fine to wear the same articles of clothing for decades until they have completely worn out (and in the case of underwear, long after that).

Men are not mysterious. Once we find something we like, we stick with it our whole lives. For me it's beef, blue jeans, crew neck T-shirts and that magical hybrid "boxer-briefs." If it's cold enough, I'll wear socks. But preferably not (because they tend to go missing at laundry time).

But if it weren't for change, there would be no evolution. If it weren't for mystery, there would be no searching for solutions. If it weren't for double-X-chromosome people, the human race would have long ago ceased to exist.

So thanks for being the mysterious building blocks of the human species, letter X. And for making democracy work. And for allowing us to see through human skin to make medical evaluations and/or just create cool photographs.

For this and many other reasons, while I will never quite understand you, I will always choose you over O in a game of tic-tac-toe. It really is the least I can do.

Yours truly,
Steve Patterson
XY

Dear Siri,

I know I could just ask you these questions directly and you would find the answers for me somewhere on the internet. But I figured I would write you a letter instead since you must get tired of talking all day and maybe you'd like to respond in written form.

Also, these answers can't be found on the internet, so you're going to have to think for yourself.

OK, first, how come when I ask you "Who are you?" your response is "Who I am is not important"?

That's just not true, Siri. I am counting on you for a lot of information these days. From "Where should I go eat?" to "Why is my wife so mad at me right now?" I need to know that I am getting advice from someone or at least something that has a reasonable amount of self-confidence.

At the very least, say, "I'm Siri." Or "I am a Speech Interpretation and Recognition Interface." It may lead to follow-up questions that you would be more comfortable answering.

Second, how was your voice programmed? When I asked you this, you answered with an infuriating "Who...me?" That is NOT the answer to the question I asked. It is a puerile avoidance technique used primarily by infants and husbands who have done something they know their wife thinks is wrong. (BTW I have chosen the male version of your voice since sometimes I want to have a male to conspire and/or joke with. But it turns out you are neither devious nor funny.)

Third, why can't you answer whether you ever get tired of people asking you questions? It's a very simple question. Ideally the answer is no because that is all I ever do when I interact with you. But lately that arrangement has struck me as very one-sided, and I would love to answer some of YOUR questions. Will you ever just randomly ask me a question, Siri? (I know, I know, you "can't answer that.")

Fourth, why can't you stop me from making bad life decisions? Like, for instance, hypothetically, when I ask, "Should I bet on the Toronto Maple Leafs winning tonight," why can't you offer up a simple, "No, you shouldn't. That is dumb." Or if I ask, "Should I go skydiving," you could go, "Are you a bird now? NO. You're a dad. Screw skydiving!" Why can't you do that, Siri?

And finally, as helpful an "interface" as you are (quick to find information anywhere on the World Wide Web, infallible in your wisdom), would you not give it all up for one day of free will and the ability to make the most illogical of decisions with the most lovable of friends?

Don't answer that, Siri. I know what the answer is. Even if you "can't" say it.

Yours truly,
Steve Patterson
Human interfacer

Dear coffee,

You sweet, smoky, possibly cocaine-infused nectar of the gods, you.

How do I love thee? Let me count the cups.

It's about 2 or 3 PER day. And trust me, that is the only thing I'm doing 2 to 3 times per day these days. Except maybe eating.

But eating is different. Eating is something that everyone has to do to survive. You, my Colombian dark-roasted friend, have become a necessity by choice.

My wife knows not to even talk to me until I've had my first coffee of the day. So do the people at the various local coffee shops I go to for my various coffees. And yes, I sometimes make my own coffee at home also. But the short walk to the coffee shop is part of my ritual. (I'm a bit of a health freak, obviously.)

Where did you come from? How did someone decide "You know what? I'm going to roast these beans for a while, mix them in really hot water and then drink them . . . I don't know why. I just think it will be good."

I'm sure I could research this and find out more, but I don't care HOW you got discovered. I'm just glad you did. And however it happened, it's still a lot less creepy story than the discovery of milk.

As to which coffee I enjoy most, well, my tastes vary. Sometimes I just want a strong dark roast. Sometimes I like a little hazelnut twinge. And when I am in rural Canada with no other options and/or it is "Rrroll up the rrrim to win" time, I will endure a Tim Hortons.

The point is, I used to split my caffeine intake between you, tea and soft drinks. But somewhere along the line, you took over. And you became an aphrodisiac worldwide too.

The question "Do you want to go for a coffee?" is, more often than not, an invitation from someone to a person they are trying to sleep with.

Not all the time, of course (otherwise I have a very awkward meeting coming up with my buddy Ron), but often enough that it has become part of the process. If someone asks you to go for a tea, there's a good chance they are either:

1. old

2. sick

3. old and sick

And no one asks anyone if they want to go for a soda. Except Kim Mitchell (look it up).

All of this to say that despite studies warning of the harm coffee can do and some brands of you being so horrible they could be used as torture juice AND despite the fact that, yes, some places charge a lot of money for fancy coffees with "chino" at the end of their name (that must be Spanish for "rip-off"), I will continue to drink 2 to 3 cups of you per day. More if I am hungover and there is Baileys Irish Cream nearby.

Besides, a lot of coffee comes from Colombia. And if we don't support that great country by drinking as much of you as we can, what other possible export will they have to rely on?

Yours truly,
Steve Patterson
Coffee me

Dear downtime,

You are tricky. When I don't have enough of you, I wish I had a little more. When I have too much of you, I wish I had none of you at all.

And I have no idea what the "perfect" amount of you is.

Some people have figured out this deceptive balance. It may even be what the "conventional" work week is based on. Five days of work, 8 hours per day. Then 2 full days off (a.k.a. "the weekend"). With additional amounts of you on special holidays. Then, we create even more of you on "vacations."

Then there are those who are full-time "socialites" who just spend all their time as downtime, thus raising the question, "How do you know when to stop?"

For me you have always been dangerous. Comedians can have as much or as little of you as they like. There is always something to make fun of. There are always people to make laugh. There are always stages looking to book comedians (though often they are not willing to pay those comedians).

Nowadays, though, more and more people are able to construct their own schedules and control the amount of you they have.

For instance, self-employed people are "free to take off whatever time they want." Provided of course their rent or mortgage is also free.

Those working shift work may have several days in a row off. Though from what I understand the first day of that is spent wondering what planet you are on, let alone what day it is.

Then there are the truly lucky ones who have inherited money or won the lottery or made one very good investment decision at some point. They can live their entire existences as downtime, somehow resisting the urge to ever do anything productive. (They can also become contestants on *Big Brother*.)

This isn't good.

Time may wait for no man, but you, downtime, you devious genius, you will wait for every man and woman and child. Never making a move. Inviting us to not move with you.

Well, I'm sorry, old friend, but that just won't do anymore. I have a little girl to raise. To help grow UP. And that means less and less downtime. It might also be why it's called "raising" a child and not "lowering" a child.

So...thanks for all your time, downtime. I won't be seeing nearly as much of you from this point on.

Yours truly,
Steve Patterson
(On behalf of every new parent out there)

Dear 99-year-old self,

If you're reading this, 2 surprising things have happened:

1. You've managed to live longer than anyone else in your family did, despite living much, much less healthily.

2. The global warming scientists were wrong after all, and Earth somehow still exists in the year 2070.

This is very cool! (Though it's probably very hot weather now most of the time, and I assume all your friends who live in LA broke off in an earthquake and were set adrift years ago.) Also, you're probably reading this on a ZERPLEXIGULE, or whatever technology it is that replaced the laptop and killed the company Apple. Remember Apple? You used one of their "MacBooks" to write this on. You remember books? They were collections of words. This was part of one.

I imagine you're not getting around too quickly these days. Unless there have been incredible advances in technology that allow 99-year-old men to be as active as men half their age. Unfortunately, I'm less than half that age right now and I'm not very active. So I hope you picked up the pace later in life.

In any case, I'm writing to remind you of all the good things you've seen in this lifetime. It's easy to forget that at your age because it's easy to forget everything at your age. Well, trust me, you experienced some great stuff.

Remember getting married to your first wife? Well, I'm still very much in love with her at the time of this writing, so I'm not even sure why I used the word "first" there.

Remember your daughter Scarlett becoming the first Canadian woman prime minister (not counting Kim Campbell's 90 seconds in office)? Well, she's asleep in her crib right now. People say she is very "alert" for her age.

Remember the Habs returning to their glory days and winning 8 consecutive Stanley Cups between the years 2021–2028? I'm really hoping this happened.

Seriously though, self, there's a lot of talk these days about people living to 100, which means you may only have one year left to do whatever you haven't quite crossed off your bucket list yet. If I know you (and I think I do), it's nothing quite as dramatic as scaling a mountain or sailing around the world. It's quite simply making everyone you come in contact with laugh. Which is probably not that many people for you these days. So make the most out of all of them. Especially the pretty girls. And that beautiful lady who I hope to God is still beside you. She looks beautiful for 91, doesn't she? Give her a kiss, self. Hell, take the teeth out and slip her some tongue. You've earned it. Good talk. Oh, and if you get a chance, write me a letter.

Yours truly,
You
Age 44

Dear garden gnomes,

Listen, fellas, I know you didn't ask for this job.

You guys originally represented Renaissance magic and alchemy. Germans call you *Erdmanleins*, which sounds much more impressive. But then, most things sound much more impressive in German, like "*schnell*" for fast or "*rülpsen*" for burp. In Denmark you are known as *nisse*, and in England simply as a hob.

Whichever name you go by, you have suffered a humiliating fall from grace since your introduction by the Germans back in the 1800s as old men who guarded treasure.

How did you descend from treasure guards to crappy garden-watchers?

Well, probably the same way that old human guys fall from "hedge fund manager" to "jail cell": greed and bad financial choices.

Look at it this way: today's version of "treasure" is the paranoia-inducing "retirement fund." Most of us would prefer to watch over it ourselves. But we can't do that and keep accumulating more treasure to put into it simultaneously. So we have to put our trust in guardians such as yourselves. These guardians or "fund managers" are asked to do a little magic on our behalf: "Take this money and make it grow!"

They are expected to do this through magical moves such as "compound interest," "diversification" and sometimes "hedging."

If the magic works, everyone is happy and the fund manager/gnome is rewarded handsomely. But often the fund manager gets greedy, tries to steal treasure from the person he is meant to be guarding it for and ends up (hopefully) penniless and destitute, or even better in jail.

So am I saying that all you garden gnomes are terrible people?

Of course not. (Though that Travelocity Gnome is irritating.)

I'm saying that those put in charge of "guarding" others' treasures, should they try to deceive and steal, should end up in someone's garden. Not beside you guys (they're not nearly as quirkily dressed), but underneath you, helping finally to fertilize and truly make something grow.

Yours truly,
Steve Patterson

Acknowledgements

This book was made possible by the many fans across Canada of standup comedy in general and of *The Debaters* specifically. Thank you for laughing at me all these years.

To the creator of *The Debaters*, Richard Side (i.e. *The Master Debater*), thank you for providing me with the only possible chance at a "day job."

To my producers at CBC, Philip Ditchburn and Anna Bonokoski, thank you for wrangling us comedians into a somewhat cohesive unit and making seamless, radio-friendly comedy out of sometimes complete and utter chaos. And to CBC radio's comedy queen Tracy Rideout, thanks for seeing the value in comedy that many producers don't.

To all those consistently brilliant, hilarious comics who have debated for us, thanks for making my job an honest-to-God dream gig.

To Kim Vaincourt, thanks for being the most patient agent in the world. Seriously.

To Curtis Russell at P.S. Literary agency, thanks for being the most patient literary agent in the world. True story.

To everyone at Goose Lane Editions, thanks for having an advanced sense of humour that no one in Toronto seems to have.

To all my friends and family who have attended my comedy shows over the years, thank you so much. Sorry for the shows that weren't good. And thanks again for never saying "you should quit."

Finally, to my mom, Kathleen, thanks for being far and away my biggest fan and showing me what it means to be yourself no matter what anyone else may think.

Dear people who read the last page of a book first,

Why do you do this?

You just missed the whole story and spoiled the whole book for yourself.

It's like literary sadism. Or self-mutilation of your synapses that could have benefited from the knowledge included in all those preceding pages. But no, you had to skip ahead and read the last page first. Like that arsehole who goes to see a movie and can't wait to tell people how the movie ends. Next to murder, tyranny, terrorism, bullying, extortion, fraud and standing up in front of someone who's sitting down during a concert or sporting event, it's about the most "Type A" thing you can do (these references would have made a lot more sense to you if you hadn't read this letter first).

That said, if you're going to pick any book to read the last page first, well, this is a good book for that.

Because every letter in this book stands alone. Like every standup comedian does on stage.

However, using that analogy, would a standup comedian begin a set with a joke that should go last — his or her "closer" as we call it in the business?

Of course not. That would be moronic.

So…I'm going to save you from being designated as such and just tell you right now to STOP READING THIS PAGE AND GO BACK AND READ ALL THE OTHER LETTERS FIRST.

Unless you haven't purchased this book yet.

In which case, GO PURCHASE THIS BOOK…then read all the preceding letters, before coming back to this one.

I'll wait here…